Praise for *#butGod*

"This book is about the joy of life and the justice/injustice of life. We all know that life is not always fair and as you read this book you will certainly have that cross your mind. This family has had many injustices touch their family: from the death of a child to the life-threatening accident of another. Yet joy prevails throughout this book, and the Bible tells us that the joy of the Lord is our strength. Jeremy, Emily, Caleb, and family all understand that God *is* a miracle worker, and their hope is in Him. You will feel the calm assurance that God is with you, that He knows and He cares for you from the words they write. I know that once you start reading this book you will have a hard time laying it down. It is a joy-maker and an encourager. It really is a #butGod true story."

—David and Barbara Green, founders, Hobby Lobby

"Pastor Jeremy Freeman and his family have endured crushing disappointment and heartbreak, but they've also experienced the redemptive and healing power of God. If you are facing significant challenges, Pastor Jeremy's book *#butGod* will build your faith and equip you with the strength to overcome."

—Craig Groeschel, founding and senior pastor, Life. Church; *New York Times* bestselling author

"There are some books that when you start reading you cannot put them down. *#butGod* is one of those books. This is an amazing story that will captivate you. You will laugh and cry. You will weep for sorrow and weep for joy. And in it all, you will see the amazing grace of God and His sustaining power and love for His children. The Freemans are dear friends. I am so thankful they are willing to share their remarkable journey—a journey that is not yet finished!"

—Dr. Daniel L. Akin, president, Southeastern Baptist Theological Seminary, Wake Forrest, North Carolina

"The tragedy of the cosmos is the legacy of sin and a consequence of the Fall. That tragedy also presents itself in human suffering that is simultaneously intense and inexplicable. In this book, part testimonial and part reflection, Jeremy Freeman takes the reader into his own family's experience of pain and trial. This is a very moving book written by a very thoughtful pastor, who shares with the reader his confidence that in all things God is working out His glory in the lives of believers—and for eternity."

—DR. R. ALBERT MOHLER JR., PRESIDENT,
SOUTHERN BAPTIST THEOLOGICAL SEMINARY

"Few of us have experienced anything as gut-wrenching or expressed anything as God-honoring as Jeremy and Caleb Freeman. The Freemans' story is true triumph in the face of real tragedy. Their story of love and faith in God is one of the greatest inspirations you will ever read."

—TOMMY WOODARD AND EDDIE JAMES, THE SKIT GUYS

"Gripping, honest, and directed straight at anyone who has suffered or will suffer, and that's all of us. This book is not sentimental or shallow; it gets us to hope the only way we can ever find it—not by going around heartbreak but by going right through it to the other side."

—DR. RUSSELL MOORE, DIRECTOR OF THE PUBLIC
THEOLOGY PROJECT AT CHRISTIANITY TODAY;
AUTHOR, THE COURAGE TO STAND

"The Freemans' story is breathtaking and meaningful as they share their challenging circumstances yet remain ever steady in their trust in a good and loving God. Not only have they endured unimaginable hardships and survived, they have come out the other side of their suffering with astounding joy and exuberant hope. Read this book, and see the goodness of God!"

—MICHAEL AND LAUREN MCAFEE, COFOUNDERS OF INSPIRE
EXPERIENCES; COAUTHORS, NOT WHAT YOU THINK

"It is tempting to read a stranger's account of tragedy and triumph and wonder if it is all true. Is their faith *that* genuine? Did they *really* say those things? This story *is* real. The pain described is real, the faith expressed is real, and the God holding the Freeman family together is real. I heard Jeremy declare his faith in God even while heartbroken when his son Trey went to heaven. I saw his faith in action in the hospital the night Caleb and Clayton were in the horrific accident. I have witnessed his family's influence over his precious congregation. What I have seen is a family that serves an extraordinary God. This book tells the story of the Freemans' journey through tragedy, but it testifies to so much more. It shines the light on the Source of their hope, the Lord Jesus Christ, and it points the reader to the only One who can see you through your own day of struggle. You may not be able to make beauty from tragedy, but God can!"

—DR. MICHAEL STATON, SENIOR PASTOR, FIRST
BAPTIST CHURCH, MUSTANG, OKLAHOMA

"This story will inspire you. It is a story of a family walking through pain and trauma, in need of a miracle. It is a story of life change and yes, of a miracle. In a cynical world, we need books that inspire us to once again believe God. You or someone you know needs to read this. One of my favorite phrases in Scripture is 'but God.' It reminds us that things can change when God shows up."

—MICHAEL CATT, AUTHOR AND FILM PRODUCER

"Caleb not only has an incredible story, he has an incredible heart. And I can't think of anyone better to talk about either of those than Jeremy, someone I've known for more than twenty years. Not only will you be touched by this book, you will discover the answer to the hunger so many in the world have. Now more than ever people are crying out, *But God . . . why did this happen?*, *What's next for me?*, or *When will it be over?* Caleb is living proof that God is diligent to answer."

—DR. ALEX HIMAYA, FOUNDING AND SENIOR PASTOR,
BATTLECREEK CHURCH, BROKEN ARROW, OKLAHOMA

"This is the story of a family in the fire. It has been my honor to know four generations of this family who love each other and serve the Lord. And I don't think I have ever known a family who has endured more loss, heartache, grief, and disappointment. On nearly every page of this book, you will find a family praying and persevering—two premier indicators of faith. Prepare to be challenged as you read about an extraordinary young man and his impressive parents. This book does what Caleb does—it puts the spotlight on God's faithfulness, God's power, God's purpose, and God's saving grace through Jesus Christ our Lord."

—Dr. Hance Dilbeck, president and CEO, GuideStone Financial Resources

"In #butGod, Rev. Jeremy Freeman somehow manages to convey all the emotion—the highs and the lows—he and his family experienced in the aftermath of the 2017 car crash that led to his son Caleb's life-altering injuries. Hope is a central theme throughout, but Freeman also explores concepts like surrender, perseverance, and loss through the powerful lens of faith. Those who have followed Caleb Freeman's story over the years are sure to appreciate the many details, prayers, and life lessons Pastor Freeman has shared in #butGod. Those who are new to the Freemans' story will also be inspired by one Oklahoma family's journey of miracles and their continued mission to share God's message of hope."

—Carla Hinton, faith editor, The Oklahoman

"Tragedies happen to all of us, but few people gain all that God can give in difficulty. This rare book by Jeremy Freeman gives us a front-row seat to a modern miracle. Filled with honesty and raw truth, #butGod not only tells us the Freemans' story but also gives us deep theology about how to face suffering and really live. I read this book in less than four hours because I couldn't put it down. It is a *must-read*!"

—Bill Elliff, founding and national engage pastor, the Summit Church, Little Rock, Arkansas

"It's good to be reminded that while we see to the corner, our God sees around the corner. What we see as problems or pain, God sees as purpose and potential. In his book *#butGod*, Jeremy Freeman unpacks one of the most devastating tragedies any family could possibly face. In doing so, he reveals how God took the difficulties of their story and repurposed them for His glory. And as a reader, I'm reminded that every person is either coming out of a tragedy, currently experiencing adversity, or preparing to walk through a catastrophe, and yet God's promises still apply, and I'm reminded that our God intends to use all our stories for His glory."

—JORDAN EASLEY, SENIOR PASTOR, FIRST BAPTIST CHURCH, CLEVELAND, TENNESSEE; AUTHOR, *LIFE CHANGE*, *ESCAPING THE CAGE*, AND *RESUSCITATING EVANGELISM*

"Caleb Freeman's amazing life story is a reminder that God is with us in times of the greatest tragedy and in times of the greatest triumph. I pray all those who read this powerful book will be inspired to live life for the glory of Jesus, just as the Freeman family does."

—BRIAN HOBBS, EDITOR, THE *BAPTIST MESSENGER* OF OKLAHOMA

"You were made for more than wealth and fame. In fact, you're not really living at all until you have your own personal #butGod moment like the Freeman family. Jeremy got the phone call every father dreads. His book will help you face with courage and hope those long nights and the tough days after tragedy strikes."

—JEFF STRUECKER, ARMY RANGER HALL OF FAME, PASTOR, AUTHOR, PODCASTER

"Don't play the odds when God's in the game. *#butGod* is a raw, page-turning account of the Freeman family's journey through tragedy: their monumental loss, their bottomless faith, and the complete transformation of their oldest son."

—ALI MEYER, NEWS ANCHOR, KFOR-TV; AMERICAN EMMY AWARD–WINNING JOURNALIST

"This is more than a book. This is a survival guide on how not to let what seems impossible stop you from what God says is possible! If you don't want to be inspired and motivated to make your life count, then don't read this book. If there is a calling for more in your life, you have to get this book."

—DR. ED NEWTON, LEAD PASTOR, COMMUNITY BIBLE CHURCH, SAN ANTONIO, TEXAS; AUTHOR, *BREATHE AGAIN*

"I have watched Jeremy and Emily and their children walk through the darkest valleys and prove the faithfulness of God and His Word. *#butGod* is not merely a story with a happy ending. It is a reality-based journey of people who encounter real pain and suffering and grow deeper in their love for a faithful God who refuses to leave us alone or leave us the same. It has been my distinct honor to know the Freemans and pray for them in the midst of some of life's most challenging trials when hope seemed utterly lost, #butGod."

—DR. ED LITTON, PASTOR, REDEMPTION CHURCH, MOBILE, ALABAMA; FORMER PRESIDENT, SOUTHERN BAPTIST CONVENTION

"If you wonder whether God works miracles, this is a moving testimony of God's intervention in the life of the Freeman family. I have been overwhelmed and encouraged by Jeremy's honesty and deep faith. All readers will be captured by God's miraculous mercy and care in their life journey. Take this book, read it, wrestle with it, and encounter God's grace."

—DR. HEATH A. THOMAS, PRESIDENT, OKLAHOMA BAPTIST UNIVERSITY

"Every single person needs to read this story. You will be challenged, inspired, and mobilized to live out your #butGod story. Jeremy and Caleb are the real deal, and I can't possibly recommend this book enough. Get a copy for yourself and a copy for everyone you know who needs to be encouraged."

—SHANE PRUITT, NATIONAL NEXT GEN DIRECTOR, NORTH AMERICAN MISSION BOARD; AUTHOR, *9 COMMON LIES CHRISTIANS BELIEVE*

#but
GOD

#but GOD

THE POWER OF HOPE WHEN
CATASTROPHE CRASHES IN

JEREMY FREEMAN

NELSON
BOOKS

An Imprint of Thomas Nelson

Published in Nashville, Tennessee, by Nelson Books, an imprint of Thomas Nelson. Nelson Books and Thomas Nelson are registered trademarks of HarperCollins Christian Publishing, Inc.

Published in association with the EPIC literary agency.

Thomas Nelson titles may be purchased in bulk for educational, business, fundraising, or sales promotional use. For information, please email SpecialMarkets@ThomasNelson.com.

Library of Congress Cataloging-in-Publication Data

Names: Freeman, Jeremy, 1977- author.
Title: #butGod : the power of hope when catastrophe crashes in / Jeremy Freeman.
Description: Nashville, Tennessee : Thomas Nelson, [2022] | Summary: "Pastor Jeremy Freeman shares the miraculous story of his son's 10 percent chance of survival after a devastating car accident, the darkness that nearly overtook their family, and the #butGod movement that captured the prayers of believers and brought hope and healing"-- Provided by publisher.
Identifiers: LCCN 2022012161 (print) | LCCN 2022012162 (ebook) | ISBN 9781400238286 (trade paperback) | ISBN 9781400238309 (ebook)
Subjects: LCSH: Consolation. | Hope--Religious aspects--Christianity. | Freeman, Caleb. | Traffic accidents. | Crash injuries--Patients--Religious life. | Christian biography.
Classification: LCC BV4910 .F68 2022 (print) | LCC BV4910 (ebook) | DDC 248.8/6--dc23 /eng/20220706
LC record available at https://lccn.loc.gov/2022012161
LC ebook record available at https://lccn.loc.gov/2022012162

Printed in the United States of America

22 23 24 25 26 LSC 5 4 3 2

This book is dedicated to my son and hero, Trey Robert Freeman.

I am a better man, husband, father, and follower of Jesus as a result of the seven years God gave me with you. Not one day goes by that I don't think of and miss you. I cannot wait to see you again. Until then I will run the race with the strength God has given me—just as you did—and I will finish my race with the faith God has given me—just as you did. I love you, son, and I thank God for your life and the impact it continues to have. As Jesus said, "I am the resurrection and the life. Whoever believes in me, though he die, yet shall he live, and everyone who lives and believes in me shall never die" (John 11:25–26). I am thankful that on January 8, 2013, you trusted Jesus as Savior, Lord, and Boss and that on September 1, 2013, Jesus carried you all the way home. I love knowing that you are forever alive in the presence of God. This book is in your honor, and I will see you soon.

What God has done in my heart is the greatest miracle. God took somebody who should have died and caused them to really live.

—CALEB FREEMAN

Contents

Contents

Foreword

BY DAVID PLATT

But God.

Just think of the times we see these two words together in God's Word.

Joseph, reflecting on all the evil done to him by his brothers and others, said, "You meant evil against me, *but God* meant it for good" (Genesis 50:20).

Saul was seeking to kill David, "*but God* did not give him into his hand" (1 Samuel 23:14).

When King Jehoshaphat and the people of God were in imminent danger, they received word from on high: "the battle is not yours *but God's*" (2 Chronicles 20:15).

In utter despair, the psalmist wrote, "My flesh and my heart may fail, *but God* is the strength of my heart and my portion forever" (Psalm 73:26).

And don't these two words summarize the essence of the gospel?

We were dreadful sinners, "*but God* shows his love for us in that . . . Christ died for us" (Romans 5:8).

Jesus died on a cross, "*but God* raised him from the dead" (Acts 13:30).

We "were by nature children of wrath, like the rest of mankind. *But God*, being rich in mercy, because of the great love with which he loved us, even when we were dead in our trespasses, made us alive together with Christ—by grace you have been saved" (Ephesians 2:3–5).

Indeed this is the gospel, and it is the greatest news in all the world. For all who trust in Jesus, sin may plague us, suffering may hurt us, and death will come to us, *but God* will save us fully and finally forever and ever.

Even still, it's one thing to write out these truths from God's Word. It's a whole other thing to live them out in this fallen world. And that is why I am so grateful for the book you hold in your hands. Caleb Freeman's story is one of hurt and heartache, pain and suffering, trial and tribulation. But God has turned all these things—all of them—into a story of healing and hope, peace and joy, testing and triumph. And the good news is that the same God who has done (and is still doing) this in Caleb's life wants to do the same in your life.

Now don't misunderstand. This doesn't mean that Caleb's story is a tale of tidy bows on deep sorrows or trite answers for difficult questions. I cried multiple times reading through this book as I stepped into the anguish of Caleb's story (and his family's story), not just in the past but also in the present. In the process I found myself face-to-face with sorrows and questions in my own life, family, and faith. But in the end this book led me—and I am confident it will lead you—right where we need to go. To the God who has not left us alone in our sorrows or with our questions. To the God who has come humbly to us in this world and spoken tenderly to us in His Word. "In this world you will have tribulation," Jesus said. He never promised us tidy bows or trite answers. Yet you'll never guess what his next word was.

But.

"But take heart," he said. "I have overcome the world."

These words are why this book will take you from tears rolling from your eyes to a smile spreading across your face. For you will realize in a fresh way that for all who trust in Jesus, unimaginable suffering may come our way in this world, *but God* will ultimately have the last word.

—David Platt, lead pastor at McLean Bible
Church, Washington, DC; founder, Radical;
New York Times bestselling author

Foreword

BY SENATOR JAMES LANKFORD

E very family needs hope and a future. When you turn the page, you will quickly find out that the Freeman family found themselves in multiple situations where there was no hope or future—but God.

Life is not just hard, it is confusing. Really bad things happen to really good people. Not just some of the time— all of the time. No family is immune from life's challenges.

I remember when I heard the news about a terrible auto accident involving two teenage boys on their way to watch a college basketball game. Little did I know at that moment that the boys were in a family I knew well. I also did not realize that their family's challenging journey did not begin that day; it had actually begun long before.

This is not Caleb's story; it is God's story. For families willing to open their eyes to what God is doing around them and through them, they can also see God at work in their family. Sometimes pain and the loss are so great, it wipes away the distractions from God's movement. For some the pain becomes the distraction from God's faithfulness. For the Freemans, when there was no hope but God, they saw God's love and greater purpose in the pain.

I read #butGod on a plane, which was a terrible idea. I sat in my seat weeping as—I assume—the total strangers around me tried to figure out my problem. But there was no problem; it was only grief, joy, and gratitude. Moms and dads should read #butGod and reflect on their own parenting. Students should read #butGod and reflect on their life goals and aspirations. Families should talk about #butGod and remember that no matter the circumstances of their life, "but God."

—Senator James Lankford, Oklahoma

Prologue

Caleb would say that the version of him that existed before the wreck is no longer here. That version of Caleb claimed to be a Christian, but no transformation had pushed him into full, selfless belief. Caleb describes his past faith-life as religious in a purely surface sense. He merely played the church game and went through the motions. He made the decision to be saved as a child, and we saw elements of spirituality in him, but he was quiet and reserved about his faith. His Christianity was a simple fact about who he was; he was a Christian in the same way he was a runner, although he practiced his running far more than he exercised his faith. That is, until the day when Caleb's life changed forever: the day when Caleb was *wrecked*.

There was a ringing phone.

There was running, speeding, praying.

There was searching.

There was waiting.

There was begging God.
In Caleb's brain, there was nearly nothing.

In the hospital, Caleb was declared a 3 on the Glasgow Coma Scale, which measures consciousness in a person who has sustained a brain injury. A fully awake and functioning brain scores a 15. A score of 3 indicates the patient is completely unresponsive, in a brain-dead state with a high chance of mortality. This is how things were for days that turned into weeks. Then a sudden, speedy, and miraculous awakening, followed by gradual recovery, led to the rebirth of our son.

If you saw Caleb today, he would appear completely normal at first. If you continued to observe him, though, you would discover a young man who looks as if he's on the brink of falling every time he walks. His hands shake, and he lacks many fine motor skills, such as holding a fork—but he manages. He still tries. His speech is not all that clear, and he struggles with balance and coordination. He writes letters, but his handwriting looks like that of a five-year-old. He can't drive; his reflex time isn't fast enough. Though frustrating, those physical losses pale in comparison to his spiritual gains.

Caleb is journeying through this phase of his life by faith and faith alone. He wasn't instantly healed and brought back to wholeness. This continues to be an exercise in maintaining hope and faith even when we can't yet see the results. That's what Caleb has taught us. He has been broken, both physically and spiritually, and God is restoring him. The miracle is not that he is still alive but that, through the trauma and the physical injury, Caleb actually sees his life and his purpose more clearly. A pastor friend of mine once told me there are just some things you cannot see through dry eyes. We tend to think we would see better if our eyes were dry and clear, but it is when we are broken, crumbled, and lost in desperate prayer that things make the most sense.

The essence of becoming a Christian is that you are born again; you are brought to life spiritually. Caleb is alive today in every possible way. What was dead in Caleb is now alive. He would tell anyone that he was *wrecked* physically but that he was also *wrecked* spiritually. And he needed to be wrecked spiritually so he could be rebuilt in God's image. For that, we are eternally grateful. We are all wrecked in some way or another. We just need someone to show us that redemption is possible here on earth. Thanks to being wrecked and subsequently brought back to *real* life, Caleb is that guy.

———

Like many famously gifted people, Caleb swears by his routine. His routine is a form of discipline and sometimes of survival. Much like athletes who take ice baths and vocalists who practice their warm-ups, Caleb wakes up early and the first thing he does is spend time in the Word. Quickly following that, he has a specific playlist he listens to as he worships in his room. His worship style is dynamic and powerful—sometimes electric. Caleb knows that worshipping

God involves our hearts and minds as well as our bodies. Things like lifted hands, bended knees, and animated movements outwardly express what is going on in his soul. Some people quell their actions out of embarrassment, but Caleb feels he has nothing to hide from God. Uninhibited, he stands in front of his door, blaring his music, shouting words of praise. He sometimes will even recite a monologue that he found of Tauren Wells's ad-libbing in the middle of Elevation Worship's song, "Here Again."[1] Caleb doesn't care who is asleep. He sings at the top of his lungs because that's how he gets his heart ready for the day, whether we have a speaking gig scheduled or not.

As Caleb worships unabashedly, the responses from the family vary. Sometimes members of the household put pillows over their heads and try to grab a few more minutes of sleep; other times we get up and join in. By far, Luke and Addi—our two youngest—join in the most. Addi will pop her head into our room and say, "We're going to worship with Caleb for a while. We'll be back!" Then she will tug a smiling Luke along with her. We know they'll be dancing their hearts out for Jesus. They don't have to explain a thing.

As the playlist comes to an end and Caleb finishes his first round of worship, he continues his routine. We assist him in anything he needs help with—which is not much, as he has learned to adapt his physical limitations and accomplish the tasks at hand. After he's ready, if we have a speaking gig scheduled, we hit the road.

When we get into the car, the very first thing Caleb

wants to do is pray about where we are going and what we are going to do when we get there. We do this together, asking God for guidance, praying He'll use us to do His will. Then, as I turn the key and the car rumbles to life, it's all about the worship. Again. Caleb plugs his phone into my truck's speaker system, and we worship the entire way. I have known him to sing out loud for three or four hours straight while we drive. He rocks out, lost in the splendor of our Lord. I am left to watch the road, sketch out ideas for our speaking event, and wink at other drivers who laugh at Caleb's overflowing expressions of joy.

Caleb does not like to plan what we talk about. He loves spontaneity, believing Jesus can better direct him if we leave some space. Caleb simply says, "Dad, you follow the Spirit, and I will follow you."

Caleb and I have such trust in each other and such unshakable faith in God that we are able to get up in front of thousands of people together, unrehearsed, and know without a shadow of a doubt God will use us to touch dozens, if not hundreds, of souls with Jesus' love. With that in mind, we head out onto the stage, asking God to direct our every move. Caleb is dynamic, passionate, and, man, is he funny. When the event wraps up, people often rush to the stage, hands reaching out in praise and an overwhelming spirit of commitment to Christ. That feeling of His divine presence is something I never tire of, nor is it something I can fully grasp. I didn't always trust God or believe He would heal here on earth. But I have learned through experience that our God is a kind God; a loving God; a God who shepherds us through the storm when we are wrecked, only to restore us in His perfect way—one that brings Him the greatest glory. This is the God Caleb and I get to serve as we travel the country in my truck, spreading the gospel through Caleb's story.

EMILY'S JOURNAL AND OTHER UPDATES

The first entry in Emily's journal.

Though I walk in the midst of trouble, YOU
        WILL REVIVE ME;
You will stretch out Your hand
Against the wrath of my enemies,
And Your right hand will save me.
The LORD WILL PERFECT that which
        concerns me;
Your mercy, O LORD, endures forever.
    —PSALM 138:7–8 (NKJV, Emily's emphasis)

Chapter 1

The Call Nobody Wants to Receive

FROM CELEBRATION TO DEVASTATION
IN TWELVE MINUTES FLAT

As I drove toward the restaurant to meet my sons, big fat raindrops started to hit my windshield. Each one made a loud *splat* just before it rolled down the glass and onto the hood of my car. The radio played softly as I flipped on my turn signal and guided my car into the parking lot where Caleb and Clayton were already waiting in their car. As I pulled into a spot near theirs and ran to their driver's side window, it began raining a little harder. I approached Caleb's window, and he quickly rolled it down. I smiled and handed them the tickets, drops of rain now running down my face.

Clayton and Caleb were heading to the University of Oklahoma basketball game, and I knew they'd return home full of caffeine and adrenaline. I was excited for them; I loved seeing them so pumped. The rain continued to fall, and though I don't always do this, something compelled me to say, "Be safe guys. Take it slow in this rain. Make sure to stay buckled up."

They both nodded, promising to be safe. Caleb tapped out one last text, then I gestured to remind him to put his phone in the console. He knew not to be on his phone while he was driving, so he placed it there without question.

"It's okay, Dad," Clayton called out from the passenger seat. "We'll use my phone for directions to the game."

"Okay, that's great. Have fun. I love you guys," I said, then jogged back toward my car and headed home.

About fifteen minutes later, I walked into the house, which was warm and smelled like Christmas. My wife, Emily, was getting ready to host a party for her girlfriends and was hard at work baking cookies and preparing appetizers. I planned to make myself and our younger kids scarce by taking them to see Christmas lights—to drive around town and look at all the houses that were decked out for the holiday. Just as the door closed behind me, my phone rang. I pulled it out of my pocket to see Caleb's name on the screen.

"What's up, buddy?" I asked.

"Sir, do you have two sons?" On the other end was not Caleb's voice, but that of a grown man.

My mind couldn't comprehend hearing someone's voice aside from one of my sons'. He didn't even say my name. He just bounded right into a conversation. I pulled my phone away from my ear just to make sure I actually had seen Caleb's name on the caller ID. There it was, plain as day. I put the phone back to my ear. "Who is this? Why do you have my son's phone? What is going on?"

Again, he said, "Sir, do you have two sons?"

"Yes," I finally managed, "but who is this?"

"Your sons have been in a car accident. How quickly can you get here?"

My first thought was that they had been in a fender bender, and because they were minors, they needed me to help fill out paperwork and sort out the insurance. I turned back toward the door and said, "Okay, let me—"

He cut me off.

"We just need you to get here as quickly as possible." His voice was urgent.

My heart dropped. My stomach flipped. I started to panic. "Let me talk to Caleb!" I yelled into the phone.

Emily walked out of the kitchen when she overheard the conversation. She could tell something was wrong as I continued to shout at the man to allow me to speak to Caleb. When he still wouldn't hand over the phone to my son, I said, "We'll be there as quickly as we can. Don't hang up!"

The man stayed on the line as Emily and I decided to leave the other kids home by themselves until someone could get there and stay with them. Aubrey was nine at the time and would be able to watch Luke and Addi, who were two and three. Emily sat them on the bed and said sternly, "Don't leave this house, do you hear me? Your aunt will be here any minute." She then called her sister who lives just a few minutes from us and asked her to come over right away. With the kids still on the bed, now huddled together, Emily and I rushed out of the house. I was still on the phone with the man.

As I got behind the wheel of my truck, I kept pleading, "Please, just let me talk to Caleb," into the phone. Every time I said that phrase, the man deflected. There was something he wasn't telling me. "*Please*. Just let me talk to my son!" I begged.

He finally said, "Sir, I'm not a medical professional, but I can tell you that your son is still breathing."

"What? Still breathing? What do you mean, 'still breathing'?"

At that point, an icy feeling of anguish washed over me. I feared Caleb was dead and this guy didn't want to tell me over the phone.

I handed the phone to Emily and navigated the route to the accident scene, retracing the boys' path. Emily tapped the speaker button and held the phone out as the man gave us a vague description of where they were, but we didn't need it. Traffic was backed up for miles, so I pulled onto the shoulder and stepped on the gas. Emily, who is typically the calmer of the two of us, was hysterical—coming completely undone. We were hanging on the words *your son is still breathing*, but we knew that meant things were dire. We needed to be by his side. Eventually, I pulled fully off the road to avoid hitting or sideswiping any of the cars at a standstill. I was driving in the grass and mud, my truck bouncing with each rock and pothole I hit. Cars honked at us and drivers poked their heads out of their windows, screaming at us as we drove toward the whirling lights.

Emily pulled out her phone and called her sister to make sure she'd made it to our house. Then she dialed her father and began sobbing, telling him what was happening. With my phone now in the cup holder, I was still desperately maintaining contact with the man who was at the scene. I couldn't fathom what had happened, yet my mind ran through every possible scenario. I had seen them less than an hour ago, and my phone had rung just minutes after I left them. How could this have happened so quickly? Emily continued to scream into the phone as lights from other cars and streetlights brightened our car like bursting flashbulbs. Suddenly, I heard Clayton's voice in the background of the man's phone. Was Clayton okay, or at least able to speak? I still couldn't hear Caleb, and they still wouldn't give him the phone.

Finally, we got close enough to the scene of the accident to jump out of the car and run. On foot, we weaved our way through the maze of stopped vehicles to the center of it all. As we arrived at the crash site, we were able to see our sons' crushed car, then the semitruck that must have hit them. The lights of emergency vehicles cast an eerie, undulating glow in the puddles that continued to gather rain as we tried to get our bearings. Through the chaos, I managed to see the man who was on the other end of the phone. I shoved my phone in my pocket and ran up to him. He introduced him-self, then pulled Emily toward one of the two ambulances. I would later learn that he was an MMA fighter who'd also been on his way to the Oklahoma University basket-ball game that night when he saw the accident. Something urged him to pull over and run back down the highway to see if he could help. When he arrived at the scene, he found Caleb's phone, and Clayton was coherent enough to put in the passcode. He scrolled through the numbers and found the entry "Dad." That's how he knew to call me.

As our new friend guided Emily ahead of me, she glanced over her shoulder, her eyes desperate. Emily and I had come to the same conclusion at the same time: Guiding her toward one ambulance was really him guiding her away from the other. We both knew something serious was going on in the other ambulance—something he didn't want us to see. We finally reached Clayton, pale and scraped up with a blanket thrown over him. A pulse monitor gripped his finger, and a blood pressure cuff encircled his upper arm. His tear-filled eyes stared straight ahead. He barely even registered that we had arrived. Two EMTs by his side monitored his vitals as he slipped in and out of consciousness. He didn't remember the accident at all. Over and over, he asked, "How's Caleb? Where is he?"

We kept repeating, "Clayton, what happened? What is going on?"

He looked confused, unable to piece anything together. Clayton had sustained a concussion, according to the EMTs, which was affecting his ability to connect to anything other than his missing brother. They needed to get him to the hospital, but they couldn't get out until the other ambulance was ready to leave.

As we talked to Clayton, I kept trying to catch a look at what was going on with Caleb. All I could see was a second ambulance swarming with emergency personnel. The vehicle seemed to rock as EMTs moved around inside. Then one of them slammed the doors and turned on the siren, which screamed into the night sky.

Someone yelled out to us, "You need to get to OU Trauma Center!"

The next thing I knew, we were being ushered back toward our car, and the doors were closing on Clayton's ambulance too. I felt nauseated, nearly retching as we ran. There was a much closer hospital in Norman, but they weren't taking our boys there. Knowing that OU was the hospital in Oklahoma City that took all the severe trauma cases, we began to understand just how serious both boys' conditions were.

We got back to the car soaking wet. Rain poured from the sky as if heaven and earth were mourning a loss we couldn't imagine enduring. Not again. So we flung our doors open and thrust ourselves into the truck. We were no longer concerned with what had happened or how; those thoughts seemed irrelevant now. We launched into howling, desperate prayer as I gripped the steering wheel, navigating my way around cars, driving on the shoulder, making our way to the hospital as quickly as possible. Utter chaos reigned as I drove—a collision of phone calls, desperate conversation, prayer, pleading with God, and nonsensical cries of anguish. We weren't even able to pray with words. We were moaning in unison, and every once in a while, one of us would scream, "Please, God, spare him! Please, God, spare our son!" It was the longest twenty minutes of our lives.

As a pastor, I've been with people in their final moments. I have gotten the phone call to drive to the ER, meet somebody, and pray over a loved one before they die. Emily and I had been through the loss of a child before, and I wasn't even close to emotionally healed at the time of Caleb and Clayton's accident. I was still struggling to believe that God healed here on earth. We had recently experienced so much loss, and I simply couldn't believe it in my heart. This moment required complete, unwavering faith in God. Yet my faith was weak; I felt He had chosen to do something other than what we had prayed for so many times. As we pulled up to the hospital and bolted for the doors, I braced myself to learn that Caleb's only hope was to be healed in heaven.

As the doors of the ER slid open, I yelled, "We're here for Clayton and Caleb Freeman!" The nurse at the counter asked us to wait, then ran to check with attending staff. She quickly returned to let us know that Clayton had arrived but Caleb had not. We had no idea how to force our bodies to wait. The lighting was bright and sterile, the tile floor cold and sick looking. Even the paint on the walls seemed off. Everything around us felt fake—like a movie set. Emily and I embraced, but neither of us was really there in that moment. We were each lost in our own despair.

Despite my inner struggle, my questions, and my lack of trust in Him, God showed up as if to remind us of His divine glory. As Emily and I paced the waiting room, we noticed a woman with a heavy coat and a large, billowing scarf who was there with her children, obviously enduring her own nightmare. She didn't know us, but she could sense our desperation. We stopped and turned toward her as she walked over to us. Without saying a word or asking permission to touch us, she dropped her hands on our shoulders and began to pray. As she spoke, peace washed over me. I was suddenly filled with the hope I was so desperate to find. I opened my eyes and looked at Emily. Her face was calm, her eyes gently closed. It was such a powerful moment amid the mayhem. God used a complete stranger to remind us that our son was in His hands—and that His hands were holding ours. We couldn't be with Caleb at that very moment, but with this woman's touch, we knew God never left his side.

After the woman finished her prayer and we thanked her, another woman came running into the ER with blood all over her. She ran up to us and asked, "Are you Caleb's parents?"

"Yes," I said, and Emily nodded.

"I want you to know I was with your son," she blurted out. "And I prayed over him head to toe—I'm Jalinda."

Gripping our arms, Jalinda explained that she was coming home from a funeral and saw the wreck. A certified CPR responder, Jalinda felt compelled to pull over and see if she could help. When she got there, no one at the scene was tending to Caleb because they didn't know what to do with him. He was out cold and bleeding everywhere, so Jalinda cleared his airway and made sure he was still breathing. The next words out of Jalinda's mouth nearly sent me to my knees: "God told me your son is going to live."

I couldn't imagine how much faith and trust it took for Jalinda to speak those words. It's a bold statement to make to a parent whose child is fighting for his life in the ER. I mean, neither Jalinda nor Emily and I really knew anything about Caleb's condition, yet Jalinda was led to deliver that message. I so badly wanted to believe her, but the cynic in me just wasn't sure. I was living in a mixture of fear and faith and couldn't see my way out.

Finally, an ER nurse rushed over to us. "He's here and they're working on him," she said. "In the meantime, let's get you into a more private room." She led us down a long hallway and into a room filled with purple-and-green vinyl chairs and benches. In my tenure as a pastor, I'd been in "family rooms" like this many times, whenever it was a dire, touch-and-go kind of deal. That room held no hope for me. Before the nurse left, she promised, "They'll come get you when they have an update."

Time crawled by, and people started to show up for Caleb and Clayton. They were all ushered to the family room, where we sat waiting in agony. Ours was such a small community that news travelled fast. Even the police officers called to the scene knew our family. The look on every single person's face who entered the room told us they were not hopeful Caleb would recover. Some people stayed, and some left after offering prayers and asking what else they could do. We had no answers to that question. The only One who could do anything for us at that time was God.

———

As evening slipped into late night, Emily and I settled on one of the benches with my jacket over us like a blanket. Emily drew a breath and pulled a notebook from her bag, which she typically used for things like making grocery lists.

"What are you doing?" I asked.

"God spoke to me," she said in a near whisper. "I know in my heart that Caleb is going to have a story that will help countless others. I need to write down everything that has happened and everything that's coming. God is going to use Caleb to change the world."

I looked at her with my eyebrows knitted together.

Emily began to journal, even though she didn't know what the future held. Watching her write furiously, my body relaxed a little. God was still showing up for our family. He was letting us know He was working in all our lives—especially in Caleb's.

EMILY'S JOURNAL AND OTHER UPDATES

December 21, 2017—Written in the ICU

Oh God, let this become Caleb's testimony. Let him rise from the ashes of defeat. Let him rise to declare your victory. Let him awaken with a message burning in his soul and a boldness to share it with everyone who is placed in his path.

In Jesus' name . . . amen!

Chapter 2

Bubble Boys

MONSTERS AND MIRACLES

E mily has three siblings—a sister, Jeannie, and two younger brothers, Matt and Dan. Emily and her family enjoyed a happy, uneventful life before her brothers were born. They grew up in Oklahoma but spent part of every summer in Colorado. They spent tons of time outside, playing, hiking, and fishing in the summer months. Emily was always active and loved the sport of tennis; she seemed naturally gifted and had a competitive streak that drove her to excellence, even from a young age. Her father taught her to play tennis and was coach to her and her sister. Later on, the sisters became high school state champion doubles partners.

Emily's grandfather was the pastor of their church in Seminole, Oklahoma. His favorite verse was Nahum 1:7, which says, "The LORD is good, a stronghold in the day of trouble; and He knows those who trust in Him" (NKJV). Little did Emily's family know, as they memorized those words, how much they would cling to them later.

Matt was the first boy born into her family. They brought Matt home from the hospital just like any other baby, excited to welcome him into their life. They'd had two healthy girls who progressed and grew as expected, but Matt was different. He did not grow much, nor did he put on weight. He also continued to get sick, even more than the one kid in every family who seems to pick up every single bug that's going around. Matt was sick *all the time* with high fevers and a cough he couldn't seem to clear. Eventually, his pediatrician diagnosed him with failure to thrive. The family needed a solution. Fast.

Back in the eighties, there was an oil boom in Oklahoma, which drove billions of dollars to the state. More money meant there were more resources fueling research. Hence, there was a special team of doctors at the Children's Hospital of Oklahoma (now the Oklahoma Children's Hospital) doing research on immune deficiency in children. Somehow, Matt's case was brought before one of the doctors on the research team. He called Emily's parents and asked, "Has anybody checked to see if this child has a functioning immune system?"

Elated at the possibility for answers, Emily's family brought Matt to Oklahoma City to see these doctors. After a series of tests, sure enough, they discovered Matt did not have any immunity. He was born with something called SCIDS, not to be confused with SIDS (sudden infant death syndrome). SCIDS stands for severe combined immunodeficiency syndrome, which leaves those who suffer from it without the ability to fight illness of any kind. Many variations of SCIDS exist, but Emily's family's is X-linked—meaning if the mother is a carrier, it is likely to be passed from mother to son with a 50 percent chance of transmission.

Upon Matt's diagnosis, they immediately isolated him, putting him in a bubble of protection like the main character in the film *Bubble Boy*. As her family focused on Matt's healing, Emily's carefree existence came to a halt.

The first treatment offered to babies suffering from SCIDS is a bone marrow transplant. It is ideal to transplant marrow from a family member who is a perfect match, but if that isn't available, a half match—typically a parent—will suffice. Emily's dad donated bone marrow to Matt not once, not twice, but three times, and on the third time, the transplant was successful. Only then did things begin to shuffle back to a new version of normal for the family.

———

After the pain SCIDS brought to Matt and the rest of the family, Emily's mom and dad decided definitively against having more children and sought to prevent it from happening; but by the time Matt was diagnosed, much to their surprise, Emily's mom was pregnant with Daniel. Learning it was a boy created immediate fear and tension, and it led to an abundance of fervent prayer. Even though doctors encouraged them to abort Daniel, that option was not on the table for Emily's mom and dad.

Thankfully, the family now knew enough about the disease to test early for it. Sadly, the amniocentesis, which is the testing of the amniotic fluid using a hollow needle, revealed that Dan had inherited SCIDS. The family was thrown into preparation for another battle against the disease that seemed to plague every boy born to the family.

When Dan arrived, he went immediately into isolation, and this time Emily's mom donated bone marrow. Because they knew much earlier that Dan had the disease, they were able to start treatments right away. Thanks to this, Dan began to thrive much sooner than Matt had been able to.

Unfortunately, the battle with SCIDS does not end in infancy. Throughout their lives, Matt and Dan had to diligently take treatments to remain healthy. They received what is called IVIG (intravenous immunoglobulin) once a month to help boost their immunities. The treatments helped them live much like any other kids. In fact, the boys were medical miracles. The professionals agreed they shouldn't have been alive at all—especially Matt, whose problems went undiagnosed for so long that he suffered long-term side effects.

Emily, Jeannie, and their parents did their best to support the boys, but as they got older, SCIDS continued to evolve. Matt always had problems—some significant. Common illnesses that someone with a normal immune system would easily recover from often brought Matt to his knees. For example, when Matt was in college, he developed a debilitating wart virus on his feet. He couldn't get rid of these warts, no matter what he did. Finally, doctors at a nearby hospital tried an experimental treatment that cleared up the virus. But that was long after the virus had stolen so much from him.

Dan was always the healthier one, but around 2014, he got sick as well. He contracted the norovirus, which is extremely contagious and causes vomiting and diarrhea. If you or I get it, we would become sick but likely overcome it fairly quickly. Because of his SCIDS, Dan battled the norovirus for three years. He was miserable, sometimes going to the bathroom dozens of times a day. They tried everything possible to help him, but nothing seemed to work. He simply dwindled down to nothing. Despite the devastating effects the virus had on his body, Dan remained faithful to the Lord. He led his family to trust in God, even if he wasn't fully healed on earth. In 2017, Dan's body succumbed to the disease and the havoc it had wreaked on him. He finally experienced his full healing with his Lord and Savior, Jesus Christ.

A month later, the night before Caleb's accident, we gathered with Dan's widow and his three children to remember Dan, preparing ourselves for the first Christmas without him. Little did we know that the very next day, our whole life would unravel again. We could never have predicted that we'd be wondering whether we'd need to prepare for a Christmas without our beloved son Caleb as well.

EMILY'S JOURNAL AND OTHER UPDATES

December 20, 2017—Written in the ICU

For we were so utterly burdened beyond our strength that we despaired of life itself. Indeed, we felt that we had received the sentence of death. But that was to make us rely not on ourselves but on God who raises the dead. He delivered us from such a deadly peril, and he will deliver us. ON HIM WE HAVE SET OUR HOPE THAT HE WILL DELIVER US AGAIN. You must also help us by prayer, so that many will give thanks on our behalf for the blessing granted us through the prayers of many" (2 Cor. 1:8–11, Emily's emphasis).

We are on our way. Driving frantically through the rain. We are desperate not knowing what we will find and imagining the very worst. We are not allowed to see Caleb. But Clayton seems to be okay. That's good. But Caleb. What about Caleb? This can't be happening. I need to see my son!!! They say something about a semitruck. No. Where is he? BUT GOD.

Racing to the trauma center. We beat the ambulance and we are searching frantically for any word or any sign of our boy. A lady in the ER with her family. She sees our pain and our panic. She walks over and she lays her hands on us and she prays . . . and there is calm. Her words are true. Her words are comfort. Her words point to Jesus. They provide peace. It doesn't make sense. Thank You, Lord. BUT GOD.

Chapter 3

Sir, We Need a Miracle

WHEN YOUR HEART IS RIPPED OUT

After several hours, they finally let us see Clayton. The hospital was so crowded that he was lying in a bed in the hallway. As we sat by his side, he tried to remember what had happened, but he was groggy and still didn't have a clear picture of the crash. From Clayton's bedside, I could see the room where Caleb was being treated. My anxiety went through the roof as I watched doctors and nurses scurrying in and out of his room.

Why can't we just go in and see him?

Finally, a nurse walked close enough to me that I was able to catch her attention. I called her over and asked, "Ma'am, can I talk to you for a second?" I pulled her into a small hallway and asked for an update on Caleb.

With eyes filled with terror, she said, "Sir, has nobody talked to you yet?"

"No, nobody has talked to me!" I responded, louder than I meant to.

"I don't know how to tell you this," she said quietly, "but at this point, your son needs a miracle. We need a miracle."

That was the only time I felt like I was going to pass out. I sat down on the floor and leaned my head against the cold wall. Tears rolling down my cheeks, I wriggled my phone out of my pocket. The screen's bright light stung my tired eyes as I tapped out a text to our family that said, "The doctors and nurses are telling us that Caleb needs a miracle." Then I typed in two words: *but God.*

I didn't even know what I was saying at that point. But I knew that if God didn't step in, this thing was done. It was my way of saying to them (and to me), "God has to do this. He will have to intervene."

I looked up from my phone, and Emily was at the end of the small hallway waving me over. We had to say goodbye to Clayton for the moment and head to another floor where Caleb was being taken. We rode the elevator clutching hands, then hurried out and found our way through the maze of hallways to Caleb's room.

When we got there, the neurosurgeon came out of Caleb's room and gave us grim news. "Sir, your son has suffered a severe traumatic brain injury called a diffuse axonal grade III brain injury. On the coma scale, he is currently a 3 out of 15, which means he has barely any brain activity at all."

In disbelief, Emily and I nodded in unison.

"I'm just going to shoot straight with you. The swelling on his brain is severe. We will do all we can to help him, but I just want you to know we do not expect him to live through the night. We have to take him to surgery right away."

In that moment, Emily and I were surprisingly stoic. I had already had my time of collapsing, and Emily had so much faith and trust in God that she took in the news without coming undone. We simply retreated to the waiting room together and began to pray. I begged God to heal Caleb on earth. I wasn't ready to let him go home yet.

God came through.

That night, they drilled a hole in Caleb's head to drain the fluid off his brain. Caleb survived. The next twenty-four hours were just as critical, but he survived those too. Then, the next sequence began.

"He's lived forty-eight hours, and that's good," the doctor said. "But your son, as you know him, will never be the same again. He won't call you dad. He won't be able to walk, talk, or eat again. In all likelihood, he will be on the ventilator and feeding tube for the rest of his life. Ninety percent of patients with a diffuse axonal grade III brain injury don't wake up."

All I could think of was that phrase I had so mindlessly typed: *but God*.

EMILY'S JOURNAL AND OTHER UPDATES

December 22, 2017—Written in the ICU

We believe in the power of prayer. But we are experiencing that power in a mighty way. The knowledge that thousands of people are praying around the clock all over the world for our son is both humbling and oh so encouraging. We are in a constant state of prayer. A constant state of dependence. Knowing we have no power on our own. He holds the power of life and death. He is our only HOPE and so we cry out day and night without ceasing.

Chapter 4

What We Meant When We Said "I Do"

SIGNING UP FOR A COMEDY AND GETTING A TRAGEDY INSTEAD

Emily and I met at Oklahoma Baptist University. She was a freshman, I was a sophomore, and we were both on the Welcome Week steering committee. For our tenure at the school, our committee was in charge of putting on orientation for the new freshmen every year. Emily and I hit it off from day one. We were instantly comfortable with each other and were able to share both the light and heavy stuff with ease. I think it's like that with a lot of couples who have that soul connection. You start recognizing parts of yourself in another person—familiar details encased in someone wholly new to you. I looked forward to talking to her every time I knew we'd be together. I still remember the way my heart jumped when I'd round the corner and see her coming my way.

When I finally asked Emily out, I asked her to go to church with me. I had to know from the get-go that we could share a relationship in the Lord. As it turned out, we could. Of course, we had our awkward moments with hand brushes and blushed cheeks, but that comes with every beginning. There was something so special about sharing that time with Emily, worshipping side-by-side, getting to know how proudly she embraced her faith in God and prioritized time with the Lord.

Not long after that first trip to church, Emily and I

started dating seriously. Our early relationship was a series of ups and downs. We didn't start off slowly with silly dates that eventually developed into a relationship. Neither of us wanted to waste time on something that didn't have the potential to turn into something bigger and stronger. We were young and were trying to figure out whether this was a forever thing or not. We broke up for a short period of time before realizing we really did want to be together for the long haul. I always say that God used that period apart to make us stronger as individuals because when we got back together, we were in it for better or for worse.

We learned early on that life is full of disruptions. We both had a certain maturity because of our pasts, so we felt that God had prepared us for some of our future challenges. We got married in February 1999 when Emily was finishing her junior year of college. We were both shocked when Emily became pregnant with our first child, Brittany, in September 1999, which meant Emily spent her entire senior year in college pregnant. With that pregnancy came questions and concerns that forced us to grow up quickly. Looking at Emily's family history with SCIDS, we knew we could be in for some major obstacles.

We had Emily tested and, sadly, found out she was a carrier. Because of what she and her family had been through due to the disease, Emily was strong and had a deep trust in the Lord. After all, her brothers had survived into adulthood with the odds stacked against them. What reason did she have to believe God would abandon her now? We knew we needed to find out early if the baby was a boy or girl so we could prepare ourselves. That's when we found out it was a girl and breathed a sigh of relief. We didn't have to worry about treatment plans, illness, and preparation for the worst while hoping for the best. Instead, we got to enjoy the delicious anticipation while setting up a nursery in our small apartment and buying baby clothes, a stroller, and diapers.

When Brittany arrived, she was as cute as can be. Though tiny, she was perfection. There is no way to describe the feeling of your child grasping your finger for the first time, or watching your wife become a mom. That moment when it goes from just the two of you to your own family unit is something that can't be replicated. I never knew I could love so much. And, man, was I about to learn just how far my heart could stretch.

Just a few months later, despite our best efforts (really, I swear), Emily became pregnant again. This time, with a boy. Emily and I knew we had to go through the amniocentesis to make sure everything was okay. Emily squeezed my hand tightly in the dimly lit procedure room as the doctor used an ultrasound wand to guide the long, thin needle into her uterus through her belly. We waited for what seemed like ages for the results, but the waiting paid off in a big way when we found out that our son, Caleb, was healthy. He had not inherited SCIDS, which felt like the biggest relief in the world. We threw a huge party with our friends and family to celebrate our healthy boy.

Emily gave birth to Caleb 364 days after she gave birth

to Brittany, making them "Irish twins." Once we saw his beautiful face, we knew our family was complete. When my parents brought Brittany to the hospital, Emily and I basked in the glory of our new family and expressed gratitude to the Lord. Brittany clambered into the hospital bed with Emily, who cradled Caleb. As we sat together as a family, everything felt absolutely perfect.

When we went home from the hospital, Emily and I decided it was time to stop having children. We had been so fortunate to bring two healthy children into the world that we didn't want to press our luck. But, over time, our faith and trust kicked in, as did our desire to expand our family. We began to think SCIDS was simply skipping a generation—which our doctor told us could happen. The more we prayed about it, the more we felt like God wanted us to have more children.

About eighteen months later Emily got pregnant again, this time with another boy. We went through the now-familiar routine of the procedure room, the hand squeezing, the sonogram wand, the hollow needle, then the waiting. Only this time, things turned out differently. Our son, Clayton, was infected with SCIDS. That's when our life took a massive turn. Knowing the doctors in Oklahoma had been God's hands for Emily's brothers, they were the people Emily trusted most and believed should manage Clayton's care—but they had moved to California.

At the time, I was a youth minister at a church in Arkansas. We had two small children, and we now found ourselves uprooting our family. Clayton was born in January 2003, and medical interventions began immediately. Together, we'd go to Los Angeles for seven months to be near the children's hospital where Clayton would receive treatment, which began with a bone marrow transplant as soon as he was born.

Brittany was not a perfect bone marrow match, and neither was Caleb, so I had to be the donor for Clayton as a half match. In a series of painful procedures, I donated bone marrow and stem cells for his treatment. Then, after the transplant was complete, Clayton had to go through a round of chemotherapy to make sure his body didn't reject my cells. There's always a possibility that the body will fight cells that aren't a perfect match, so chemotherapy is used to suppress the fighting between cells. Clayton did amazingly through these procedures. It was hard to watch him go through the treatments, but Emily and I felt God's steady hands guiding us through it all. As a family, we spent as much time in prayer as we possibly could, begging for Clayton's healing. Finally, in July of that same year, we were able to bring him home to Arkansas.

———

After having Clayton, Emily and I were definitely done having kids. Having more posed too great a risk. I scheduled myself for a vasectomy, and Emily and I used double protection in the meantime.

One day I came home from work, and Emily said, "I've been hesitant to tell you this, but I'm pregnant."

I was like, "What!? How is that even possible?" The news blew my mind. I even thought, *Who have you been with, lady?*

We came to believe that the Lord wanted us to have another child even though we had done everything within our ability to stop it. When we found out we were having another boy, we prayed and wondered aloud, "Maybe he will be healthy like Caleb?"

So, with our baby boy Trey nestled in Emily's body, we went through the same procedure once more, only to find out that our beautiful boy was not healthy. Trey had SCIDS just like Clayton did. This time, we found some well-qualified doctors who practiced in Dallas, which was closer to our home since we had now moved back to Oklahoma.

Not long after, we found out our daughter, Brittany, was a perfect match for Trey. When you have a perfectly matched sibling, the treatment becomes a lot less complicated and chemo isn't necessary. Brittany donated bone marrow in Dallas in 2006. When Trey was born, he seemed completely healthy. Though he was positive for SCIDS, he seemed okay. All the same, he received the bone marrow transplant, which his body took in just as easily as we had hoped and prayed it would.

For six years, Trey lived a normal, healthy life. During those years, God used Trey to open our hearts to having one final child, who we believed strongly would be a girl. From a human standpoint, it did not make sense for us to have any more children, but God gave us a supernatural peace. In 2009, Emily and I had our fifth child, a baby girl we named Aubrey. Little did we know how special she would be and how much we would all need her. With Brittany, Caleb, Clayton, Aubrey, and Trey healthy, it felt like we were living the dream, just like any other family. We were able to put SCIDS out of our minds for a while and just watch our kids grow up.

In our house, kickball is *the* family sport. Trey was the all-time Freeman family kickball pitcher. He'd pitch the ball like a grown man, sending it hurtling toward home plate. Whoever was up would kick it as hard as they could, but Trey would catch it more often than not. He was undoubtedly the kickball champion of the group.

Over the years, we stayed active as a family. Emily and I both played sports growing up, so we liked to remain physically fit. We loved riding bikes, swimming, and playing volleyball, baseball, and basketball. We went to games and various sporting events, all of which we played and watched intensely since we're so competitive. In the summer, when the kids were out of school, we'd visit Colorado and spend weeks hiking, which Trey loved so much. In colder months when skies turned gray and leaves fell from the trees, we'd spend time together indoors. We'd sing worship songs together as a family, cozying up on the couch for movie nights with bowls full of popcorn and mugs brimming with hot chocolate. Life felt amazing, but sometimes, right when you settle in, things throw you for a loop.

———

Six years after Trey received the donation from Brittany, he began to develop fevers that would not go away. After seeking answers from local doctors and specialists, we ended up back in Dallas with Trey's original immunologists. It turned out that Brittany's cells had begun attacking Trey's cells without clear cause. The doctors' best guess was that a virus kicked the fight into play, but watching Trey suffer was brutal and almost more than I could bear. In 2012, Trey needed another bone marrow transplant, again from Brittany since she was a perfect match. This time they gave Trey chemo to wipe out his system, ridding him of old cells that would fight the new ones. The hope was to give him a fresh batch of healthy cells that would eliminate the other problem. They were hopeful that the bad cells would never come back. But when they did, they came back with a vengeance.

Once the bad cells came back, doctors tried many different ways to suppress them and give Brittany's cells a fighting chance. We encouraged them to do everything humanly possible while we prayed and trusted that God's will would be done. After what seemed like endless procedures, treatments, and therapies, we came to the end of the road in terms of what was even possible. Doctors finally recommended a third transplant in hopes of starting over again and gaining some ground.

On the third transplant, the goal was to find another donor who would match Trey since Brittany's cells were not doing well in his body. We had a bone marrow drive at our church, desperately seeking anyone who could help. Sadly, Trey never got healthy enough to endure a third transplant.

———

Emily's sister, Jeannie, had two sons, and both had been born with SCIDS. The older son, Brady, had lived a normal life thus far, but Toby, who was born the year Trey was sick and fighting for his life, needed a bone marrow transplant. The results of the transplant at first looked good, but about thirty days later, Toby's health started to decline. Toby only lived eighty-five days after the transplant. His lungs collapsed from the chemotherapy, and he died in the loving arms of his parents as Emily and I circled around them in love and prayer. I can still remember my brother-in-law holding his son in his arms, and in tears declaring, "The Lord gives and the Lord takes away. Blessed be the name of the Lord." All this happened while Trey was in the same hospital, just a few doors down, fighting the same battle. I will never forget going into Trey's room and telling him that his cousin, my nephew, had died. Trey was only seven years old at the time, and with tear-filled eyes he said, "Man, if Toby died, maybe I'll die too."

This was one of those moments I knew I'd never, ever forget.

Not long after, Emily and I were in the hospital with Trey, and he was struggling. Emily and I stood over his bed and began to pray together. As we sat with Trey in front of the Lord, I remember saying a prayer with tears rolling down my cheeks: "God, just do with Trey whatever will bring You the most glory."

When we got done praying, Emily looked at me and said, "Did you really mean that? Do you really want God to do what brings Him the most glory? That could mean the opposite of what we really want . . ."

If I had to be honest, I didn't really mean it. I prayed something that I didn't mean. There are three "isms" that we all battle: narcissism, the love of self; hedonism, the love of pleasure; and materialism, the love of things. All sin can generally be traced back to love of self, love of pleasure, love of things. For the rest of our lives, we will be combatting these ideas. God doesn't tell us to love ourselves; He says to deny ourselves. God doesn't tell us to love pleasure; He says it's okay to enjoy creation but to worship the Creator. Material things are not bad, but when those "material" things are human beings we love with our entire being, life can get tricky. Although we want our lives and the lives of those we love to bring Him the greatest glory, it's hard to know that His glory isn't always put on display with sunshine and rainbows. Sometimes it's revealed with a storm that wrecks you.

Two months later, in August, Emily's mom died. She had been battling cancer, and I had to tell Trey that another family member, his grandmother, had stepped into eternity.

I led my nephew's funeral, I led my mother-in-law's funeral, and I feared I'd soon have to lead Trey's. It was a terrible time in our lives, but who you are in those awful times reveals who you really are. Even in those dark moments, God brought beauty from ashes as people came to know the hope of Jesus Christ through our losses. At both funeral services, people began to place their faith in Jesus and follow Him. Only God can take something so heartbreaking and breathe life and hope into it.

When I look at my life with Emily thus far, I count the struggles and I feel proud that we have used them to strengthen our marriage. When you have kids, it's easy to let routines, activities, meal preparation, cleaning, etc., become the main focus. When that happens, investing in each other is no longer a priority. But Emily and I have realized that when tragedy strikes, you don't have a choice. You are forced to your knees. You are forced to define and focus on what really matters. And as much as we struggled at this time, Emily and I had five beautiful children—Trey, Clayton, and the ones we worried about least, Brittany, Caleb, and Aubrey. And Caleb was our family's miracle boy.

Caleb is the only boy born to Emily or her sister who did not have SCIDS. Clayton has it, Trey had it, and their cousins Brady and Toby had it. Caleb was the only one we never had to worry about medically. Caleb is human; we knew he'd face the normal challenges of life, but we didn't think we'd have to worry about him like we did his brothers. He was the one in the family who would be free from tragedy and trauma—until he wasn't. The accident stole that from Caleb and from our family. That reality amplified the stress surrounding the accident exponentially, but Emily and I drew closer, seeking strength from each other.

Emily and I have always believed that the goal of marriage is oneness with each other and oneness with God. When you get married, two people become one, creating a bond that—when nurtured—only grows stronger with time. Through our shared struggles, Emily and I found that suffering could either push us together or pull us apart. There is no in-between. Successful couples who face trials such as these don't just survive; they thrive. Couples who thrive in the face of challenges feel the suffering while continuing to fight for their marriages. We each need our own intimate relationship with God, but also a relationship with God as a unit; these bonds look different, each with their own unique qualities. Thankfully, God allowed the trials in our life to help us love each other better.

Don't get me wrong. Emily and I are human. We are sinful. We've had our share of ups and downs and continue to have them to this day. There have been tears, heartbreak, and moments of weakness along the way. But those trials have allowed us to share a deeper and more meaningful love between us. Our bond has grown *because* of the struggles we've endured, not *in spite* of them. We no longer fear tragedy or trauma. We know when it strikes that we have each other's backs, and, most importantly, that God has it covered. We thank Him for that strength. We desperately needed it as we headed into the unknown, battling our son's catastrophic brain injury.

EMILY'S JOURNAL AND OTHER UPDATES

December 23, 2017—Written in the ICU

Mark 4:37-39: "And a great windstorm arose, and the waves were breaking into the boat, so that the boat was already filling. But he was in the stern, asleep on the cushion. And they woke him and said to him, 'Teacher, do you not care that we are perishing?' And he awoke and rebuked the wind and said to the sea, 'PEACE! BE STILL!' And the wind ceased, and there was a great calm" (Emily's emphasis).

There is a storm raging inside my son's body, but the same God who calms the raging sea can calm the storm in Caleb. BUT GOD.

Caleb looks more like my Caleb today, and though he is heavily sedated, he still moves. Each movement is like a taste of what is to come. I am ready. Soon, Caleb. Soon. God is on the move. I know He is. He is coming to awaken you . . . to call you forth. Soon. BUT GOD.

Chapter 5

Life, and How It Longs to Be Lived

THE PRESS FOR PLEASURE AND PEACE

The week following Caleb's first forty-eight hours in the ICU was agonizing for me. I found myself pacing the floor, unable to sit, desperate to jump in and heal my son, yet helpless to do anything at all. I oscillated between prayer and all kinds of emotions with God. How could He do this to me? How could He have taken Trey and continue to allow more severe heartache in our family? Who was this God I'd once treasured and loved so dearly? Who was this God I'd worked my whole life to serve? Who was this God I led so many to worship?

My life became a series of questions that I tried to answer but couldn't without a God to lean on. It was as if the earth I'd stood on my entire life was crumbling beneath my feet, pulling me toward its molten core. No matter how hard I clawed at the disintegrating rock and soil, I couldn't pull myself up.

I was falling.

My own turmoil was directly contrasted by Emily's peace. The Lord had breathed relief into her and set her on a mission to record Caleb's story. God had assured her that Caleb's story had a far greater purpose than we could see in the ICU, and Emily quickly and dutifully obeyed. She'd sit and scribble notes as I paced the floor. It was the perfect metaphor for our relationship—I am high-strung, and she is chill, calm, and laid-back in every situation. Emily is our family's anchor. Once she got that peace, she never once doubted. God just began to carry her.

On day four in the ICU, I was pacing as usual. I was now living in sweats and sneakers. When I walked the hospital floors, my shoes would catch on the tile floor and trip me. That small misstep would send adrenaline coursing through my already exhausted body, causing my heart to race and my pulse to rise. Nothing was okay.

On day six, I left the hospital's accommodations—a hotel just down the road—and rushed back to the hospital, only stopping to grab coffee and a muffin in the lobby before heading up to the ICU. Because of Caleb's fragile condition, Emily and I were only able to be with him one at a time. It was impossible to process what was going on—how our healthy Caleb had ended up connected to the conglomeration of tubes, wires, and machines that were keeping him alive.

On this day I was feeling extra anxious. My knees bounced as I stared ahead, lost in thought—lost in the past, lost in our future. I met Emily to exchange places. Her eyes were tired, her lips pursed, yet she still maintained her air of complete calm as she jotted notes. She looked away from her notebook and caught my eye. "What are you thinking about right now?" she asked, placing her hand on my knee.

"I'm just . . ." I paused to swallow, fighting the lump that had formed in my throat. "Is Caleb going to make more progress?"

"Jeremy, God has preserved him for a greater purpose than what we can imagine."

"I so badly want him to get back to running and playing basketball. I want to see that version of him again. I can't let him go."

Emily leaned into me. "Jeremy, do you think God preserved him to play basketball again?"

I averted my gaze. I wasn't ready to think about why God preserved him, or whether He really did preserve him at all; things were still so touch-and-go. I was working through my own belief in what God was going to do in Caleb's life, and I was jaded. I *still* wasn't seeing an ounce of proof that God did heal on earth, since I'd only seen Him heal in heaven. Don't get me wrong; I always believed His ability to heal by calling people home was miraculous, but I prayed there was another way. I needed to find a way to believe God could still do miracles on earth.

I turned back to Emily. She'd begun to scribble in her notebook once again. I was filled with gratitude to be with a woman who remained steadfast in her faith amid what felt like impending doom. Just looking at her reminded me that even in moments of crisis, I have a firm foundation. I have my wife, I have my family, and I would find my way back to faith in the Lord somehow. I placed my hand on her knee and said, "I love you."

"I love you too," she said, the corners of her mouth upturned—not a smile, but as close as she could get to one at the time.

———

Although Emily was typically the calm, collected one, at some moments she needed me and I was able to hold her up. One night when we returned home for Christmas Eve, Emily and I crawled into bed exhausted. It had been a hard day. The time we'd been able to spend with Caleb was uncertain and traumatic, and we'd gotten used to that, but we were both growing weary. We spent our days hearing progress reports, listening to conjecture, and running over different scenarios with surgeons, specialists, doctors, and nurses. The waiting game was exhausting. For now, all we had were guesses.

That night, Emily tossed and turned. Christmas was the next day, and although we tried to make time to celebrate with our kids, we could not be fully present while Caleb was fighting for his life. Every part of that season had been a huge downer. Emily rolled toward me, her eyes filled with tears. As soon as her eyes locked into mine, the tears spilled over and she began to sob. Emily has so few moments like this, it took me a second to get my bearings. She was fearful, she was broken, she was unable to catch her breath as she cried. In that moment, I felt the spirit of God inside of me say, "Pray."

I began to pray over Emily, and I'm telling you that God entered the room. He was right there with us, His arms around both of us as I held Emily close. It was the first time since the accident that I'd clearly felt His presence. There have been countless times on the other side; I've been weak, and Emily has been strong for me. But on this night, I was able to be a pillar of strength for Emily.

———

Many American Christians want life to be easy. We want lives of calm, soaking in His glory, enjoying every day until we are called home. But God doesn't necessarily call us to a life of ease. In the book of Matthew, Jesus explained that we must take the narrow road and enter through the narrow gate. The wider road, the one that is easiest to travel, is the road that leads to destruction. We want the wide road to lead to life, but it is the narrow road that leads to peace and life because that is where we meet God. The family room in the ER, the waiting room in the ICU, and the springy bed in the hospital hotel have all been stops on our narrow road. And it was on that narrow road, time and time again, when Emily and I showed up for each other and God showed up for us.

The beauty of our suffering—especially in friendship, family, and marriage—is the complexity it brings to relationship. When suffering enters the picture, we must bind together and find strength we didn't know we had. When one is weak, the others must be strong. Not only have I experienced this with Emily, but also with my children.

In many ways, we feel like God called our family to suffer. Even though we've all had moments when we've wanted to collapse, we never want to waste our suffering. We want to use our suffering for the glory of God because so many people need that encouragement in their own suffering. No matter what, God meets us in our struggle and carries us all the way home. Life here on earth is simply a journey of faith, trust, and infinite growth. We are passing through, but we are not home yet.

EMILY'S JOURNAL AND OTHER UPDATES

December 25, 2017—Written in our home

It's Christmas. Christmas with Caleb and without him. Jeremy and I went home on Christmas Eve to be with Aubrey, Luke, Addi, Brittany, and Clayton. We kept it very simple with presents and Santa gifts. It was nice . . . until it hit me. *It* was the realization that Caleb was not with us at Christmas. I had presents ready for him and stocking stuffers. Gifts he could not open. The pain and panic flooded into my mind and heart and I felt totally helpless against it. BUT GOD.

At that very moment, God used my husband to speak truth powerfully. He holds me and begins praying words that I know are true and that the Spirit means for me. And the Prince of Peace whispers so powerfully in my ear. And that peace floods into every part of my body, and there is calm. The calm restored. God reminds my heart and persuades my soul.

He is working, but it's not just about the work He is doing with my son. It's so much more. He is working in so many others, including myself. So many others who are following the Facebook page who may be reading these words even now. The promise from Psalm 138 was not just for my son, but for many. He is reviving hearts, He is perfecting lives, He is changing people, and it is all for His glory. He will complete His work in the exact moment which glorifies Him most.

Chapter 6

Even If

WHEN GOD UNFURLS THE
UNTHINKABLE IN OUR LIVES

n December 2012 following Trey's diagnosis, we brought him to Children's Medical Center Dallas. Our home, filled with our other children, was in Oklahoma, so each week we'd trade off staying with him in the hospital. We did the best we could to fill him with our love. Devastatingly, the time soon came when we had to admit that—without a miracle— Trey was not going to overcome his battle with cancer, which had come as a result of SCIDS. It was an impossible task to interact with Trey in any way that felt "right" when we could see God's plan unfolding but Trey could not.

On January 8, I happened to be the one who was home in Oklahoma while Emily was in Dallas with Trey. At about 11:00 p.m., my phone rang, and of course I panicked, thinking the worst had happened. Breathless, I answered. On the other end of the line I heard Trey's cute, raspy voice saying, "Dad! I'm a Christian now."

"What?" I responded. There was no "hi" or "hello"—just "I'm a Christian now. My spiritual birthday is January 8." That was all I heard. I then heard some shuffling as he handed the phone to Emily.

Emily explained that Trey had struggled to get comfortable that night. He was having terrible abdominal pain because of the cancer and the chemo. That night, exhausted from the pain, Trey wanted to go to bed about eight.

Whenever Trey slept, we slept; so as per usual, Emily settled herself in the bed by the window, praying as she stared out into the darkness before drifting off to sleep.

At about 10:00 p.m., she woke up and instinctively looked over at Trey. Trey looked like a little man to her, wise beyond his years. He was gazing up at the ceiling while leaning back on his pillow with his hands behind his head. Emily said quietly, "Trey, are you okay?"

He said, "Yeah, but could you come lie down with me?"

Emily went to his bed and lay by him, and they started talking. Up to that point, we didn't talk about death with Trey. We'd steered around it because we didn't want him to be afraid. That said, we did talk about the Lord a lot. He was a pastor's kid and was raised in church, so he was accustomed to open conversation about our faith.

That night, as Emily and Trey settled in, Trey said, "Mom, am I going to die?"

Emily inhaled sharply, taken aback. She gathered herself and replied, "Trey, you are not going to die until God's done with you on this earth."

"But I'm not a Christian," he responded. Obviously, he was connecting deeply in that moment to some things we had talked about with him for many, many years—never about him, but about our faith in general.

"Well, Trey, do you want to be a Christian?" she asked.

"I do," he said, turning toward her.

Without skipping a beat, Emily walked him through the gospel.

"Do you understand that you are a sinner?"

"Yes, I do."

"Do you understand what Jesus did for you? He died for you and rose again. Do you believe those things?"

"Yes."

Emily finally got to a point in the gospel story when she simply said, "Trey, Jesus needs to be the Lord of your life."

As a six-year-old, Trey didn't understand what the word *Lord* meant.

"It's kind of like Jesus is your boss," she said. "You are asking Him to be your boss. You are giving Him control of your life."

"I need to ask Jesus to be my boss?" he asked, tilting his head.

"That's right, Trey."

"Okay, Jesus! You're the boss," he said.

Emily laughed. Trey couldn't wait to call me and give me the news. It was one of the proudest moments of my life. I was so emotional, I nearly dropped to my knees. That was January 8, which we will forever refer to as "Boss Day" because that was the day Trey asked Jesus to be the boss of his life.

As a parent, you are always careful with your kids because you want to be sure they are making a real decision, not one that is inadvertently manipulated by you. From January to August, that idea of Jesus being the boss stayed with Trey. For example, when Trey didn't want to take his medicine, we'd say, "Trey, who's your boss?"

He'd say, "Jesus," and he would take his medicine.

Trey became the little boy evangelist in the hospital. He'd talk about Jesus with reckless abandon. He didn't have the reservations many of us Christians have from fear of accidentally putting someone off by talking to them about our faith. Trey bragged about his boss all the time and never hesitated to ask his care providers whether Jesus was their boss. This sparked in-depth conversations for Emily and me about faith, different belief systems, and more, as Trey opened the doors. Seeing my son carry out gospel conversations with adults made me so proud. In those moments I found myself in awe of the way our world's most innocent beings draw near to the Lord so quickly.

Caleb and Trey were super close. Trey loved all his siblings, but he always, always, always wanted Caleb to be with him in the hospital. Caleb spent as much time as he could with Trey, playing games, reading comic books, and just talking. Little did Caleb know God was using Trey to prepare him for his own journey, which he would embark on just five years later.

———

Almost exactly one year following his cancer diagnosis, on September 1, 2012, the Lord called Trey home. In the same hospital room where Trey declared Jesus to be his boss, our whole family surrounded his bed. Trey's body was worn-out—his skin gray, his face gaunt—but he was with us mentally. For a second time, he asked the question.

"Am I going to die?" Trey whispered into the room.

There I was, a pastor—the man who was supposed to have an answer. Instead, I dropped to my knees and let my head fall into my hands. I just didn't know what to say to our son who was lying in that bed, slowly being called home.

God spoke plainly through Emily. "Trey, you are not about to die," she said. "You are about to really live."

There was a collective, quiet sniffle. The rest of the family tried to keep it together in this moment when loss was inevitable. Yet, in this space where tragedy was slowly creeping toward us, reaching its icy hand into the room, warmth wrapped itself around us. Together, we were able to explore the depths of our faith as we witnessed God, in real time, entering the picture. He seeped into every corner of the room, offering comfort as He gently—gingerly—took someone we loved. Trey exhaled for the final time, and his spirit broke free from a body that had steadily, but aggressively, deteriorated. As Trey left us, there were soft sobs and quiet moans as we collectively collapsed onto Trey's body. We would miss his sweet, colorful presence in our lives, but we *knew* his spirit was safe. He was now home and whole. Our worst day was Trey's best day!

We never say that September 1 was the day Trey died; we say that's the day he began to really live. We know he is in God's presence and that his body is healed in heaven. I imagine him running and playing, enjoying all the joyous things he loved before illness crept in and made him weak. Without a doubt, Trey is *really living*, which has become huge for our family too. We wanted Trey to stay here on earth with us as we prayed for his healing and salvation—and that's exactly what God gave us. No, God did not answer our prayers the way we wanted Him to, but God healed Trey in heaven, and one day we will be with him, laughing, roughhousing, and playing kickball like crazy.

Although we are grateful for all God has done in our lives, it was hard to accept losing Trey, and it has been equally as hard to keep living. Trey was bigger than life, and when the Lord took him home, it left a big hole in our family that we still feel every day. God alone can help us learn how to live again. Slowly, He is doing that, but life as a minister means that I spend a lot of time masking the pain. It's hard to minister to people when things are going well, and it's doubly hard to minister to them when I need ministry myself. I have learned to put myself aside and to hold Trey in my heart as I counsel and minister. I allow his memory to support me as I help others face challenges and urge them to plunge deeper into faith. All the way from heaven, Trey, my seven-year-old boy, is my pillar of strength. I have come to see his passing as one of the greatest tests my family and I have faced. To us, that is proof that we are meant to endure one day at a time and do His work to the best of our ability.

Someone once said to me, "Anyone God uses mightily, He tests thoroughly." The more I think about that, the more I notice that anybody God ever uses significantly is tested tremendously. You can't name a single person in the Bible

God used who wasn't tested. Why? Because that person does not exist. And the ultimate example is Jesus. If anybody was perfect and had reason enough not to be tested, it was Jesus. Yet, He was tested in the most significant way possible. God uses hard things to grow you, to refine you, and to help you to worship Him. Sometimes the greatest measure of faith is still believing when you don't get what you are asking for or when you do get it but it looks different from what you'd hoped.

After Trey passed away, I tried to approach the situation with acceptance but did not know how to grieve. I know there is no right way, but my heart was aching in ways I couldn't imagine a human being surviving. Trey's room was the focus for so much of my pain. It was this space, frozen in time, that held memories I couldn't imagine soiling. I wouldn't dream of letting anyone sleep in his bed because it was *his*. To admit otherwise felt like a betrayal.

But God, in His infinite wisdom, had plans for that bed.

When Trey was sick, I noticed a little boy in our church I didn't recognize. After seeing him week after week, I began wondering who his family was. Emily and I started asking around, and it turned out his name was Andrew. He was being fostered by an elderly woman in our congregation. As we got to know him, he loved hearing about Trey because he and Trey were the same age. But the Lord called Trey home before Andrew could meet him. Still, from the way Andrew talked, you would think he and our son were best friends.

About six months later, Emily came home one day and said, "Hey, maybe we are supposed to adopt Andrew."

"Emily, no," I said. "There is no way. We can't do that. We don't have the space."

"But maybe we are supposed to," she replied.

We started praying about it, and I couldn't believe how quickly my heart softened. Emily and I both began to feel God's gentle presence nudging us toward adoption. It wasn't long before we began the approval process to become Andrew's adoptive parents. But we hit a snag. We discovered the system doesn't work that simply. You can't just pick out a random kid and say, "Hey, I think I'll adopt him." You have to go through a long process and be selected by the state. We were devastated that we couldn't go through with the adoption, but Andrew is still in our lives to this day. And the seed that was planted by our desire to adopt Andrew germinated in ways we had never imagined.

Through our attempts to adopt Andrew, we started and finished the process of becoming foster parents. Not long after, I got a phone call from the Department of Human Services (DHS). I put the phone on speaker and waved Emily over to participate in the conversation. The DHS agent said, "Hi, Mr. and Mrs. Freeman. Look, we have some interesting news. The mom of the little boy in your church you wanted to adopt has had another baby."

Emily and I looked at each other with wide eyes.

The man continued. "Would you be interested in

fostering this child and maybe even adopting him sometime in the near future?"

I spoke up. "Yes! Yes, of course we will do that."

Not long after, we brought a three-month-old baby into our home. We named him Luke. It was magical to fill Trey's room with such light and love; now so much life existed in a room that had reminded me of the opposite. We were thrilled to have a new member of the family bringing laughter and joy where there had been none for so long. The funny thing was, as happy an ending as that would have been to our story, God wasn't done bringing little gifts to us.

As Luke reached his first birthday, we got another call from DHS. Andrew and Luke's mom had had another baby—a little girl whom we would name Addi Joy. Luke, Addi, and Andrew are all related. They have the same mom but three different dads. DHS tries to keep siblings close to each other, so Luke and Addi are considered what is called a kinship adoption. Not only that, but they are both Andrew's half-siblings. Even though we didn't understand why we could not adopt the way we wanted, God was working on His master plan. In that, God took a loss and turned it into a home for two kids and a place in our hearts for Andrew. We love them all so much. They did not replace Trey, but they are a part of God's healing in our lives. Talk about God bestowing beauty instead of ashes.

EMILY'S JOURNAL AND OTHER UPDATES

December 29, 2017—Written in the ICU

Thankful! As this day comes to a close, I find myself being so thankful, which seems strange given our circumstances and the fact that our oldest son is lying in a hospital bed in the ICU . . . yet I am thankful. BUT GOD.

I'm so thankful for a God who became flesh and dwelt among us so that we could have a relationship with Him and eternal hope in Him. I'm so thankful for our family. For all that God has done in our lives to prepare us for such a time as this, that we may reflect His glory to a watching world. I'm so thankful for the peace of God and the Prince of Peace who carries me along and fills my heart continuously. I'm so thankful for how God has opened the eyes of my heart to see what He sees and value what He does. May I be His hands and feet. I'm so thankful for friends and strangers who have held us up and continue to be used by God to sustain us through this trial. I'm so thankful for prayer . . . the sacred privilege to call upon the name of the Lord and to cry out to Him. Its power is changing me forever. I'm so thankful that God is working and I'm so thankful for the things He has allowed me to see. I know there is so much more He is doing that I CANNOT see. Just imagine the day I behold it all and the veil is removed. I'm so thankful for the lives He is touching through Caleb and through me. Being an instrument of the Lord is a humbling, mighty, and awesome privilege.

Chapter 7

Modern-Day Miracle

ACTS 27:1–28

It had been a full two weeks since the accident, and our family found ourselves on a slow creep forward. There was little change in Caleb's condition, but we were seeing small—miniscule—signs of improvement. The drain they placed in Caleb's brain never had to be used. The doctors inserted it knowing that with Caleb's type of injury, there is always a first area of swelling caused by the body's immediate attempts to protect the brain. However, after that is cleared, a secondary area of swelling needs to be taken care of. Caleb's intracranial pressure never got above 30, which is remarkable. Then, instead of climbing, it slowly started coming back down. There was no medical explanation for this, which gave me some measure of comfort and hope. I began to turn one thought over and over in my head: *Perhaps God really does heal on earth.*

Like any parent would, I desperately sought signs that the Lord was present, doing His miraculous work in Caleb's life and in ours. The thing about signs is the harder you look for them, the more difficulty you have seeing them. When you search, *everything* becomes a sign. From a leaf turned over to a penny on the sidewalk, all represented a sign that Caleb would either heal or be called home. I was living in a blizzard, squinting to see what was right in front of me the whole time. And once I relaxed and managed to get myself into a place where I trusted in Him, even if the trust was fleeting, messengers showed up to bring inner peace.

In those early days, my phone blew up constantly. I had taken to keeping it on silent a lot of the time so I could focus on being in the moment with those who needed me most. Our family was lucky to be receiving such incredible support from our church family, friends, and community, but it was hard to balance remaining present and keeping everyone updated. I couldn't keep up with all the communication, so I responded to texts and Facebook messages infrequently at best, typically ignoring them until they piled into the hundreds.

One afternoon, my phone buzzed as a text came in, and I happened to be in a place where I could take a look. The text was from a pastor named Blake, from a church in Edmond, Oklahoma. Although I knew Blake and considered him a friend, we did not talk that often. That's how many pastor friendships are though. We see one another at meetings, events, and conferences, and we build up a support network for times of need. Typically, it's a prayer here, words of comfort there, but Blake's text was different. He wanted to come to the hospital and see me; he had something to share. I shook my head and texted back, "This is just not a good time. You can share it with me later."

Blake was gentle but insistent, telling me he needed to see me as soon as possible. At this point in the journey, we were only letting our family and close friends into the ICU to see Caleb, but there was something in me that felt I needed to hear what Blake had to say, so I finally agreed to his coming to the hospital to visit.

Several hours later, moments before I received a text from Blake letting me know he'd arrived, Caleb's blood pressure dropped. That meant there was scurrying and hustling around Caleb's ICU bed as doctors and nurses tried to stabilize his blood pressure. It didn't take long to stabilize him, but having a conversation with a pastor-friend after something so alarming was not what I desired to do at that moment. My heart raced and my clothes were soaked with sweat, yet I made my way to the ICU waiting room to talk to Blake.

As I walked in, Blake struggled to his feet. He was about forty years old, had sandy brown hair, and wore casual clothes. He was clearly physically uncomfortable, on crutches, and explained that he'd just had hip surgery. As we walked back to Caleb's room, he said, "Man, I know it's strange that I insisted on showing up here, but when I was praying this morning, something so crazy happened I had to come. There have only been two times in my ministry when God has spoken to me so specifically. Once was about a young lady who had cancer, and God told me to tell her family that she was going to be well. I was so scared to deliver the message, but I did what God asked. Sure enough, she was healed."

"That's awesome, man," I said, my stomach now in knots.

"I heard about the accident and immediately added Caleb to my prayer list," he continued. "This morning I was praying for Caleb, and God confirmed in my heart that your son is going to live."

I didn't know what to say, so I nodded, trying to hold back the tears.

Blake then pulled out his Bible and began to read some obscure text out of Acts 27. The passage is about a shipwreck, and Blake read it stoically, finishing with a line I'd completely forgotten existed: "There will be no loss of life among you, but only of the ship" (v. 22).

I chewed the inside of my cheek, tears now hot behind my eyes.

Blake said, "When I read that, it was as if God was saying Caleb is going to live. The only thing you are going to lose is the truck. You are not going to lose your son."

A tear rolled down my cheek.

People had been reading us Scripture, sending us verses, and reminding us what the Bible says with short summaries ever since the accident, but something was different about Blake and his delivery of this message. As soon as he finished speaking, I felt like God Himself had spoken that truth into my heart. My body relaxed; the tension released. God was present. My son was going to be okay. *The only loss will be the ship.*

With the knots in my stomach releasing one by one, we opened the Bible, laid it on Caleb, and Blake read the story in Acts over Caleb. Together we prayed, allowing our hearts to believe fully, without doubting that God was going to heal Caleb. Despite the whirring machines, the beeping alarms, and the squeaking of nurses' shoes on the tile floor, I knew my boy was still in there and would return to me— even if it was in a modified form.

The peace I felt was breathtaking. I needed to share it with my other children. As soon as Blake left, I ran from the ICU into the elevator and rode two floors up to where our other children were with Clayton in his hospital room. I must have looked completely crazy when I ran in, Bible in hand, and said, "Guys, God has spoken to us clearly from His Word. I have to read this to you right now—you won't believe it."

Together, around Clayton's bed, we read Acts 27:1–28. This became our tradition, reading the entire section almost every day over Caleb. Now Caleb can quote almost the whole thing; in fact, he woke up from the coma knowing the passage because we read it to him over and over and it stuck somehow. Even though he could not respond in the coma, he was hearing us, and more importantly, he was hearing God's Word.

I thank God for Blake, who made the trip to Caleb's bedside despite his own physical discomfort and nervousness about stepping into such an intimate place with us. God sent this man to deliver us His promise so we could hold on to it in the days when things didn't look very promising. Just as I'd almost stopped searching, that strong, life-altering delivery of God's comfort dismantled my worry. I suppose, if nothing else, I've learned that miracles are like the headlights of an approaching car. Sometimes you don't see them until they wreck you.

EMILY'S JOURNAL AND OTHER UPDATES

December 30, 2017—Written in the ICU

So take heart, men, for I have faith in God that it will be exactly as I have been told" (Acts 27:25).

The days are filled with a storm of watching numbers, listening to doctors, stabilizing pressures, and trying to make sense of it all. And in the midst of this storm, there is a calm that is not easily explainable. Floods of tears and crying out are accompanied by peace that we cannot understand. BUT GOD.

Chapter 8

The Long, Winding Road

OKLAHOMA, COLORADO, NEBRASKA, HOME

The beginning of our journey through the medical system was arduous, and with every step, we learned just how long and tedious Caleb's recovery would be. Sure, we knew about the medical system from our experience with Trey, but illness and injury couldn't be more different. With an illness, you set treatment plans to journey through one at a time until either the patient gets better or you've exhausted all options. With injury, you have endless paths, all of which are unique depending upon the specifics of the injury and the patient's overall prognosis. Our path to recovery began in the neuro ICU in Oklahoma and cascaded from there.

The ICU has multiple levels where patients with injuries on all ends of the severity spectrum are treated. Caleb was in the critical ICU for about three weeks. During his last week in the hospital in Oklahoma, he was able to "step down," or move to another ICU floor where patients were not as critical. While it was hard for us to move Caleb out of the ICU because of the tremendous care and individual attention he received there, we knew it was time for the next step. Even though Caleb wasn't responsive, communicative, or even conscious yet, getting out of the ICU was at least progress toward the next chapter in his life, whatever that was going to be. The care we received in the hospital was fantastic on every level. Even though most continued to believe Caleb would not recover, we desperately clung to the promises God had spoken into our hearts. We trusted He was leading and guiding those caring for Caleb.

For the entire week Caleb spent in the regular ICU, we obsessively observed him. Although we believed God was with us, it was hard to feel His healing hands when it seemed the medical team was not optimistic. No matter how hard I tried to maintain the strength of my faith, it remained like the reading of a heartbeat on a monitor, constantly rising and falling. Although it can be very lonely and frightening in a hospital room, God continued to send people to encourage and pray with us. Those people gave us so much hope and reminded us that God was there, holding us up. In one instance, a respiratory therapist, a man from India, came into Caleb's room and said to us, "I'm a believer in the Lord Jesus Christ, and I can tell by this room that you too are believers. May I pray for your son?"

I nodded, and the respiratory therapist prayed over Caleb, bringing us so much peace.

Then, the first nurse assigned to us let us know she was also a believer. God sent believers left and right to offer comfort and support, and it wasn't just doctors. One man whose son had been paralyzed showed up just to pray with us and encourage us. In fact, there were many like him who God sent our way, and each one seemed to come at just the right time—#butGod!

Not long after Caleb was moved to the regular ICU, he was moved out of the hospital in Oklahoma altogether. It seemed we were swiftly approaching the time when the hospital felt they'd done all they could for Caleb and it was now our job to figure out the next steps. We needed to find a longer-term solution for Caleb's care and rehabilitation. We scoured the internet and asked as many people at the hospital as possible for recommendations. We didn't care where the facility was; we just wanted the best possible place for Caleb.

After narrowing our list of recommendations, I visited three hospitals—two in Houston and Craig Hospital in a Denver suburb. My daughter Brittany went with me to visit Craig. As great as all three hospitals were, we wanted Caleb to be somewhere we knew he'd choose on his own if he were able. After seeing Craig, there was no doubt in my mind that Caleb would want to be there, and Brittany agreed without hesitation.

Denver is a place filled with young, active folks who love extreme sports. It is a popular place for mountain climbing, skiing, snowboarding, hang gliding, and other X sports—all of which come with a high risk of injury. Craig has a ton of experience rehabilitating young, athletic people, and Caleb was a sixteen-year-old cross-country star. We loved the fact that Craig wasn't a place that specialized in only one type of treatment for one level of injury. Craig rehabilitates people with all kinds of challenges, whether they be behavioral, cognitive, or physical. Their main objective is to help prepare patients for their futures and encourage them to live as independently as possible—which was all we could hope for.[1]

Once we chose Craig as the perfect fit for Caleb, we prepared ourselves for disappointment. Caleb was unlikely to be admitted since he was largely unresponsive. By this time he was occasionally blinking his eyes, tracking, trying to give a thumbs-up, but it was honestly hard to tell what was real and what was wishful thinking. At any rate, he didn't meet the guidelines for acceptance. I tried to guard my heart against the pain, but I'd fallen in love with the idea of Caleb among the athletes being treated there. I pictured him slowly improving, staring out over the mountains, and spending time dreaming of what was to come. I knew the chance he'd be accepted was so miniscule that letting my mind wander to Craig was setting myself up for devastation. Every time the thought came up, I'd shove it down in fear of the great disappointment.

But God.

Somehow, by God's grace, Caleb was accepted into Craig. It was a complete shock to us; we could hardly believe it. Even Emily, who clung to her steady faith by journaling about the miracles to come, was floored by the news. We'd have to pick up and temporarily relocate our family to Denver, but we were ready to embrace it. We'd live in a small, furnished apartment supplied by Craig, and breathe in the sweet Colorado air every morning as we'd walk to the treatment facility. We'd leave the ICU behind in favor of a place that would provide the highest level of care for our son, who deserved that and more. My faith had climbed once again like the beat of a heart, only this time I couldn't imagine it falling.

————————

One big question I had was, *How in the world are we going to get Caleb to Colorado?* After much prayer and investigation, we found a company that works with families to fly their loved ones to medical facilities. They had small airplanes, and only one family member could fly along. We decided it was best for Emily to fly and for me and our oldest daughter to drive so we could get to Denver ahead of time and arrange everything.

While this was a huge answer to prayer, it still created some angst. At this point, we worried about Caleb being in the air and having an episode. Would the medical team on the flight be able to care for him? This company assured us Caleb would be safe and well cared for.

The day came for Caleb to leave Oklahoma and fly with Emily to Colorado. I had left a couple of days before with Brittany, and we planned to meet them at the hospital. Everything went smoothly, both on the ground and in the air, and Caleb safely arrived at Craig.

Walking into Craig after being in the ICU was surreal.

It still looked like a hospital—sterile, clean, minimal—but it felt different. Death did not linger in the air. It felt like a place geared toward life—and not just *life* but *quality* of life.

When Emily and Caleb arrived, Brittany and I met them, and we walked toward Caleb's room. I remember looking over at Emily, who had absolute peace and calm spread across her face. I didn't feel all that calm. Although I was still riding high, I was secretly scared they'd take one look at Caleb and realize they'd made a huge mistake. I imagined them noticing just how little brain function Caleb had and asking us to leave. Then what? Where would we go? What would we do? I was trying as hard as I could to trust God, to believe He was really in the trenches with us, to get back to the peak I'd hit when Caleb was accepted. I was beginning to realize a trend: As many moments as I had of gratitude and belief, I had even more moments of fear and doubt.

Emily and I settled into the room, filling Caleb's drawers and hanging photos as nurses got him set up. As we folded, stacked, and tacked, a doctor walked into the room and introduced himself as Dr. Spier. My stomach tied into its familiar ladder of knots as he explained he was there to conduct Caleb's evaluation.

Across the room, Emily and I sat next to each other on chairs. Our eyes were fixed on Caleb, and I fought to keep mine there. I wanted to squeeze them shut, to run away, to scream. Then the doctor pulled up a stool next to Caleb's bed. The knots in my stomach constricted even more.

"Caleb," he said, "can you look to the left?"

Caleb looked to the left.

My heart leapt.

Emily squeezed my hand.

"Caleb, can you look to the right?"

Caleb looked to the right.

My heart raced.

Emily's grip tightened.

After a few more tests, the doctor turned to us and started to describe what he believed the treatment plan should be. I struggled to contain my joy as pure serotonin coursed through my brain. God had once again intervened, placed His hands over us, and provided the miracle we needed to keep Caleb in the place where he was meant to be.

I'd love to tell you that after this Caleb made swift improvements, building on those little glances left and right until he was up and running again. Sadly, that's not Caleb's story. Just after his intake, Caleb went back to being unresponsive. Once I'd seen those glances left and right, I couldn't let go of the idea of a complete recovery for Caleb. I couldn't release my grip on the hope that we'd play basketball again one day, that I'd go to another track meet of his, or that we'd just hang out and talk again. I tried to cling to that tiny glimpse of progress, but the daily disappointment of Caleb's unresponsiveness now felt like a regression. I tried to maintain hope even though my faith was slipping through my fingers like grains of sand. I was once again in a valley, and all I had in my heart were questions with very little room left for answers.

Making matters worse, it felt as though the accident hadn't just wrecked Caleb; it had wrecked our entire family unit. We chose to move our entire family to Denver for Caleb's recovery. While being together was so good after initial weeks of separation, it was also extremely hard. There was no place of rest. If we were both with Caleb, which was often, our oldest daughter, Brittany, was with the kids. The utter chaos left me few earthly things to cling to. No family dinners, practices, sports, or even movie nights or story times. We were stretched thin in every way, but we had to fight that feeling to remain present and strong for Caleb, who needed us most.

After the initial intake and testing, Caleb was assigned a team. Like all patients' teams, Caleb's team was made up of a neurosurgeon, a neuropsychologist, a physical therapist, an occupational therapist, a speech therapist, and a team of nurses. Although nurses swapped out frequently, the key players remained the same—well, almost all of them. Caleb's first occupational therapist was so overwhelmed by the severity of his case that she didn't know what to do with him. Thankfully, the occupational therapy team leader volunteered to take the assignment. We needed someone with the confidence to walk in and not be intimidated by Caleb's condition. She was that person. God continued to provide the right people to care uniquely for Caleb.

Caleb still required around-the-clock care, which up

until then was managed by Emily and me. In the first weeks of Caleb's time at Craig, they assigned an individual to stay with him 24/7. This was a huge relief to us. Emily and I had been switching off staying with Caleb every night. As much as we wanted to be with Caleb, we knew time away—time together—was vital. In those types of situations, it's easy to spend all the time in the world with your partner and never really see them. You're so caught up in the day-to-day, moment-to-moment, you forget to stop and breathe or whisper *I love you*. On top of all this, we had five other children staying nearby with us. They were missing out on having a full family unit. They were incredible children, making sacrifices without ever complaining, but it's impossible to know the right way to parent healthy, able-bodied children when one of their siblings becomes horribly injured.

Those moments Emily and I were able to spend together and the times we had with Brittany, Clayton, Aubrey, Luke, and Addi became vital. They were like a parting of the clouds on perpetually stormy days. For four whole weeks, Caleb not only failed to improve but got worse. A common symptom of severe brain injuries is called neurostorming. This is when a patient experiences a severe stress response as a result of damage to the brain. Neurostorms come on like a flash and involve blood pressure spikes, sudden fevers, and a racing heart. The episodes can be violent and are particularly scary for those dealing with loved ones being overcome by them.

Caleb's neurostorms were brutal and had been since the beginning—yet at Craig, they seemed to come more frequently and became more violent. Not only did they involve high blood pressure and a heart rate that shot up to around two hundred, but also Caleb had all kinds of horrifying, involuntary physical responses. He wasn't like a fish out of water, flopping all over the place, but rather he moved his stiff arms and upper body in exaggerated ways. He'd tense up, sometimes locking into one position, and at other times lock into a position and then furiously switch to another. It is scary for the caregiver watching all of this. We wanted to comfort Caleb in some way, but we couldn't.

When these storms came on, my goal was to protect Caleb from hurting himself. I had the strength to hold his arms so they wouldn't flail as fiercely, but it rarely did more than give me some small sense of control over a situation in which I was completely powerless. If we were there together when a neurostorm came on, Emily was right there with me. She'd jump in by my side and, together, we'd protect our son from further injury. Those wrestling matches were long and exhausting, like clutching the edges of a tiny boat tossed around in the sea. Often after hours of struggle, the storm would fade, leaving us exhausted and once more without the version of our son we yearned to meet again.

One night when I was alone with Caleb, his neurostorms were so severe and so frequent I could hardly believe it. The thrashing, the posturing, the frequent snapping movements were so intense it was hard not to imagine his bones breaking or muscles tearing. I fought Caleb's body for three or four hours, and though I was drained, his movements were unrelenting.

At that moment, I couldn't find a shred of faith left in my body. Instead, white-hot anger crashed over me like a hungry, frothing wave ready to drag me away. I broke away from Caleb and called out, "God, all You have to do is say *stop* and this can stop! You actually have the power to make this all go away! Where are You? Why aren't You helping us?"

I was sobbing.

I was sore.

I was sweating.

I was drained.

I was frustrated.

I went back over to Caleb's bed and put my hand on him and held his arm. The moment felt surreal, as if I'd somehow wandered onto the set of a film and Caleb was the unwitting star. I looked at his face, sunken and sullen. He had been such a strong athlete, a polite and kind guy, someone sweet, reflective, and smart. For him to go from being a pillar of strength to someone downright unresponsive was inconceivable. I laid my head down on his chest and let my weight collapse onto the bed and cried out, "Wake up, Caleb. Just wake up! Come on!"

The door to our room opened, and a woman in scrubs walked in. Instinctively, I sat up quickly and began wiping the tears from my face. She placed a gentle hand on my shoulder and said, "Sir, I'm sorry to intrude. I'm not your nurse, but I was watching you on the security screen, and I can tell you are having a hard time."

I nodded, ashamed she'd seen me at such a vulnerable moment.

She continued, "I believe God wanted me to come in here and pray with you."

"Thank you" was all I could manage.

She stood at Caleb's bedside and prayed over him, me, our entire family. Her incredible faith filled me with the warm sensation of God's love. She wasn't even Caleb's nurse, but God sent her to me in my moment of weakness and pain. Her prayers didn't stop the storming that night; it took about an hour for him to calm down. Once he did, I was able to talk to Joy, the nurse, and learn more about her. I'd been too angry to see that God was with me, so He sent Joy to me in the midst of my pain, literally and figuratively.

Due to the frequency of the storms, the staff no longer wanted Caleb to sleep in a regular hospital bed. They moved him out of a regular bed and into what they call a safekeeper bed—a giant, padded square almost like a kids' empty ball pit—because they didn't want him falling out and hurting himself even more. Although we loved having the around-the-clock care for Caleb, the neurostorms scared us enough that we resumed switching off nights staying with him.

The neurostorming felt like the Goliath to our David. We wanted to beat it down, but it simply seemed too big to tackle. We wanted to fix it for Caleb quickly—to stop the beatings his body was inflicting on itself. Sadly, no good option existed. We simply had to wait for the wave to crash on the shore and recede into the ocean, eventually returning to calm seas. The doctors at Craig continuously reminded us that we had to allow that to happen on its own. The only alternative was medication that wouldn't just calm his body but also dull his mind. We couldn't let our brain-injured son be zonked out all the time if we hoped for him to make progress in other areas. The doctors had to give Caleb's body enough space to heal without dulling his senses to the extent that he wouldn't respond to therapy. The balance was so delicate.

Although they had figured out the right balance of meds, when they tried to do therapy with Caleb, not much was happening. Those first four weeks, January 15 through February 15, we were grinding every day. It was so intense. Every time they'd do therapy with him, Emily and I would watch with our arms linked, hoping and praying this time would be different. They sat him up and tried to get him to respond to commands, but he didn't react much at all. With brain injury, you look for purposeful responses, and with Caleb, there was no sign of such response.

Caleb's lack of progress wasn't just apparent during therapy. He still was not eating on his own and was being fed through a feeding tube. He had gone from a ventilator to a tracheal tube at that point, so he could be moved around more easily, but it was by no means *easy* to move him anywhere. We would get him into a wheelchair with a lift in his room and try to push him around some, but because he was so stiff and his legs wouldn't bend, it was like we were pushing him around in a recliner. The staff at Craig had to get really creative. The woman who managed patients' mobility had never seen anybody like Caleb—with his particular tone and posture. His knees were absolutely locked, keeping his legs straight. The staff created a makeshift wheelchair out of a chair, a gurney, and straps for Caleb just so we could push him around in the hospital. When we did, we also had to take his bag for oxygen and all the accessories with him, making even the shortest walk a cumbersome, clumsy activity.

Although we saw few improvements, Caleb's face was starting to look more alert. That he still wasn't responding to commands was scaring me. Our insurance company wanted to kick us out of Craig because Caleb was not improving. On every call with us, using the same canned response, they'd explain that a patient is only able to stay in a facility as long as they can justify progress. If the patient isn't making progress, they have to leave because the treatment is too expensive. Eventually, one of the agents at the insurance company said, "Listen, you're going to have to put him in some kind of a long-term care facility until he starts making progress. Once that happens, he can be readmitted."

But because Dr. Spier had seen Caleb make those early responses, and because he knew what kind of care our son would get at a nursing home, he fought hard for Caleb to stay at Craig. We were so thankful that every time Caleb progressed the tiniest bit, the improvement was charted by Dr. Spier, which meant more time at Craig.

All during this time, as Caleb was having his hardest days, we were still believing the promise that God was going to heal him. The ever-faithful rock in my life, Emily, was more certain than I was and always kept me anchored when my faith faltered. Caleb's room had become a sanctuary of hope. He had pictures and scriptures hung all over the walls and worship songs and Christian music playing at all times. If you walked in that room, you knew our family was full of strong believers, and we saw Craig as our mission field. We loved the patients and their families and would often try and find ways to minister to them. One great example is how we chose to celebrate Valentine's Day. Initially, we were in room 316, so on Valentine's Day, we gave valentines to everybody on the hallway. We wrote personal notes in them, quoted John 3:16, and signed them: "From room 316."

We wanted to stay as long as we could, but we knew our days at Craig were numbered if something much bigger didn't happen.

Then, it happened.

Brittany was with Caleb that day as he worked with his occupational therapist. During one of the exercises, the OT leaned over to Caleb and said, "Caleb, can you nod your head yes?"

As Brittany stared, Caleb slowly nodded his head.

Brittany let out a gasp, reached into her bag, and pulled

out her phone. She hit the record button, and the OT asked him to do it again. Slightly, gently, Caleb did it again. Having that moment recorded was so special, and we couldn't be more grateful to Brittany for capturing it with her phone. Because of her, our family and Dr. Spier were able to see the miracle of Caleb's first real repeated response to a command.

She was there to see him nod his head. Since Caleb's initial consult with Dr. Spier, that was the first time he had responded to anything since the accident.

Brittany definitely had the hardest time with all of this, so it was fitting that she was the one to see Caleb wake up. She had donated bone marrow for Trey, who had died. She and Caleb were best friends and she lost him. She would just sit in the empty bathtub in that Denver apartment and cry. And of course, we needed her the most. She was going to school and trying to help us by watching the little kids as often as we needed her to.

When we saw the video, we came running. Although it wasn't exactly like Caleb nodded his head and then completely snapped out of his stupor, he quickly progressed from that nod forward as if he were saying yes to everything.

After he nodded his head that day, Caleb's recovery began to look more miraculous than we ever could have imagined. When Caleb first got to Craig, 3 out of 24 was the highest he was able to score on his alertness test. Just two days after he nodded his head, therapists at Craig administered another alertness test and Caleb scored a 23 out of 24. I nearly dropped to my knees when the speech therapist turned around and let us know his score. All my prayers and my hopes were within reach. The basketball games, the laughter and conversation, the quick, graceful running—it all seemed possible now. In my heart, I apologized to God for all my doubt. My son was returning to me; I was watching Him heal Caleb on earth.

Caleb's speech therapist could hardly believe what was happening. She and the nurse got out charts so they could ask Caleb questions and he could answer. Though he was still unable to speak, the charts provided visual answers for him to point toward. She started asking questions about things Caleb would not know the answer to unless, somehow, he was hearing us when he was in a coma. Over and over and over, he answered every question correctly. He knew what year it was. He knew he had been in a car accident. He knew how long it had been since the accident. He knew what holidays had passed. Finally, she glanced at me, then back to Caleb and said, "Caleb, are you in Denver, Houston, or Oklahoma City?"

Caleb reached his hand forward, extended his finger, and pointed to Denver.

It was hard not to feel deep pangs of sorrow for Caleb as we realized he had been hearing us the whole time but was unable to respond.

Finally, Caleb's speech therapist reached into her bag, pulled out a whiteboard, and placed it in front of Caleb. She then put a dry-erase marker in his right hand, removed the cap, and said, "Caleb, can you write your name?"

Slowly, painstakingly, he scrawled CALEB.

EMILY'S JOURNAL AND OTHER UPDATES

March 2018—Written in an airplane

Those who touched His hem . . . were healed" (Matt. 14:36, Emily's paraphrase).

Lord, Father, Abba, Dad, I believe in You. I trust in You. I know You hold the power of life and death and of perfect healing. Perfect. Complete, like You. I desire it with my whole heart and every fiber of my being. All of me. You know that full well. You know every thought I have before it enters my mind. You know all my weaknesses and they are many. Hold me together as I leave pieces in Oklahoma. There are pieces in Denver. Hold me together. Only You can.

I am on a plane headed back . . . not home . . . but kind of. There are pieces in Denver, in Oklahoma, and in heaven. I can't dwell too much on them . . . I can only do the next right thing. I'm back to that. Maybe should always be that. Help me, Lord, to hold on to Your hem. Help me, Lord. You are my help. You are my all in all. You ARE!

Chapter 9

The Tortoise Becomes the Hare

WHEN HE WORKS MIRACLES

Around the middle of March, Caleb became more alert and was able to process information on a deeper level. We knew this because he could respond to more complex questions using the charts and gestures. Although he had his trach removed and the wound was healing nicely, he still wasn't verbal. He was trying, though, and he was making progress every day. We were so proud of him, but Emily and I had to admit just how taxing it was to work with Caleb. He had to learn how to live all over again—as if Emily and I had a teenage-sized infant on our hands. With the help of the team at Craig, we had to help him relearn everything from eating to standing, walking, talking, bathing, and all the basic functions he'd lost the ability to perform. Teaching a young child to do those things is tough, but children are malleable and small. Caleb was the opposite. His body was still frozen in certain places; his limbs locked, making it nearly impossible for him to do anything with a fluid motion. We were beginning to learn about ataxia, impaired balance and coordination, which caused Caleb's movements to be forced. Trying to work with him sometimes felt like working with hardened clay. There was no way to quickly mold him; the best we could do was chip away.

The doctors at Craig continued to support and facilitate healing every step of the way. Although Emily and I conducted exercises with Caleb between therapy sessions, the team built his rehabilitation plan and spearheaded the process. They helped Caleb with swallowing—which he was delayed in—so he could make faster progress toward feeding himself. They put his right arm in a series of casts to straighten it, slowly bringing it out of its bent posture. His speech therapist worked tirelessly to help him turn the sounds he was making into words. The team went above and beyond, often staying with Caleb for long shifts to make sure he was always progressing, never regressing.

The arduous process of rehabilitation and healing was harder than I thought it would be. In the moment when I saw the video of Caleb nodding, my faith was replenished, flooding my heart with His love. Although the faith was still there, I was struggling to reconcile all that had happened and what purpose God could possibly have for all this.

The steadiest thing we had at that time was prayer. Underneath all the chaos was this rock we were anchored to. We just couldn't be shaken from it. The power of prayer and what we experienced through that was huge. We didn't always want to come out of the room and talk to people, but when we did, we would just circle up and pray. We had prayer circles all the time, and that would fill us back up and strengthen us. When we went to bed at night, there were people signed up in shifts around the clock for Caleb and for our family, so we could close our eyes and know that somebody was praying. It had been that way from the very beginning. From the first night Caleb was in the ICU, our church family and friends rallied in prayer. Honestly, we had never seen anything like it. A movement of prayer began that carried us in ways we had never known. God simply enlisted an army of prayer warriors on Caleb's behalf. People would tell us they were awakened in the night just to pray. When I was interviewed the day after Caleb's wreck by local news stations, I asked people to pray for Caleb like he was their own son. I cannot tell you how many people have told me they prayed for Caleb, perhaps harder than they have for their own kids. What a gift from God that was to us.

Prayer also realigned us to see things through the Lord's eyes and not our own. Originally our prayer was, "Please just fix our son. Please put our lives back together. Please take away this pain." Then, as we prayed and trusted the Lord more, we realized it was so much bigger than that. The reason we are here on this earth is not for ourselves. It is not so we can be comfortable and live an easy life. It is to make a difference for the kingdom. So, if this is how God is going to do that in my life and in these circumstances, how can I get on board with that?

Our journey became more of a missionary journey. We ministered to people because God had put us in our situation. God could heal Caleb anywhere and through anyone, but the reason we were right where we were in that moment was so we might possibly change somebody else's eternity. This physical stuff is temporary. Even if He fully restored Caleb, that would still be temporary, but God might use us and our story to change somebody's eternity. Prayer definitely gave us the right perspective as we waited for Caleb's continued healing.

I wanted our prayer circle to be as big as possible. I tried to post updates and prayer requests on social media as often as I could. Around this time in March, we asked for prayers for faster and stronger swallowing, that he'd become more intentional with his mouth through exercise, and that the casting process would work well for Caleb's right arm.

I also begged for prayers for vocalization and clear, visible signs that all his therapies were working. My hopes were fading for the conversations I yearned to have with Caleb and the sports I longed to play with him. I didn't know any other version of Caleb and didn't want another version of him. I wanted my son back. Little did I know that I would not only get him back, but also I'd get him back in a form that was impossible for me to imagine. Our Caleb would return to us as a version of himself God created specifically for His purpose.

———

Finally, as March was drawing to a close, Caleb began to use words again, but those words were garbled and tough to understand. He spoke slowly and had a nearly impossible time getting words out—but man, was he rocking what he was able to do. His speech therapist worked with him especially hard on regaining his ability to make *r* sounds. Words like *try* and *worship* were especially difficult for him.

The word *try* would come out like *toa* and *worship* would come out like *orca*. His tongue had been weakened from so much stagnation during his coma and after that he needed to rebuild the strength. Emily and I had to become fluent in "Caleb," a language unique to our guy.

Soon, those words and clumsy sentences became concise statements. Our conversations were slow, but we were patient, allowing Caleb to set the pace and tone. The more Caleb spoke, the clearer it became just how transformative the experience had been for him.

One day, not long after he started speaking again, Caleb made his first emphatic statement. Painstakingly, he said, "I know God is going to use this in my life. God allowed this and I just *know* He's going to use this."

"We're so proud of you," Emily said, reaching for his hand.

Over the coming days, Caleb started asking if he had wronged anybody because, if so, he wanted to make it right. He wanted to tell anybody he had failed that he was sorry. I couldn't believe the maturity he was modeling at age sixteen. Most kids in a situation like his would not be thinking about anything other than themselves and their own healing.

I was also surprised to learn that Caleb was extremely concerned about the truck driver involved in the accident. He said, "None of this is his fault. I want him to know that I'm sorry and that Jesus loves him." As early as he could talk again, what came out of Caleb's mouth was filled with the Holy Spirit. This unshakable faith was a gift from God to Caleb, but it was also a gift from God to Emily and me. Here was our son, in the midst of recovering from a traumatic brain injury, teaching his pastor dad to trust God even more.

———

A news team from Oklahoma had followed Caleb's entire journey, starting with the accident. Ali Meyer, a TV news anchor in Oklahoma, had a passion for Caleb's story and was the one who covered it for the station. One day in early April, Ali called and let me know that News Channel 4 wanted to bring a team to Colorado to check up on Caleb and film an update to the story. More specifically, they wanted to interview Caleb.

I hesitated and told her I needed to get back to her. I was worried about Caleb's ability to handle the interview. Once he began talking, Caleb's words returned quickly, but his speech was still slow and hard to understand. A simple conversation would take hours, but I didn't care. I loved talking to Caleb, hearing about the entire experience from his perspective and about his renewed relationship with Christ. However, talking with dad is a totally different audience than a camera crew filming a segment that would be seen by thousands or millions. Emily and I decided to talk to Caleb's speech therapist about it, and despite our concerns, she encouraged us. She let us know that Caleb could absolutely do it if we could have the questions sent to us ahead of time.

Not only were we worried about his ability to speak, but we were also worried that Caleb might say something inappropriate. As is typical with this type of injury, Caleb had regressed to behaving like a small child, then an adolescent boy, then, eventually, back to being a teenager—a teenager with one heck of a sense of humor that was sometimes a little (or a lot) inappropriate.

The news team was quick to get things rolling. Within two weeks, they were in Caleb's room in Colorado setting up for the interview. Emily and I stood in the back of the room behind the camera crew, watching nervously, praying Caleb would be able to handle what was to come. My palms sweating, I reminded myself just how much practice Caleb had put into this and how prepared he was—and as soon as the lights went up and Ali started talking, Caleb nailed it. He answered every question just the way he'd practiced. Then, just as I'd gotten my pulse to slow and my breathing to return to normal, I realized in horror that Ali was closing with a question that wasn't on the list.

"Caleb," she began, her head tilted. "If you could go back to December 19, 2017, would you change anything?"

Oh my gosh, I thought. *That's such a deep question for him. How is he going to answer?* I looked over at Emily, who had the same look of panic on her face. We froze, waiting for what would come next.

We should have known better than to worry about Caleb.

"No," he responded. "I wouldn't change it at all. It was God's plan, and I would never change God's plan." Even though his speech was slurred, he was speaking with such faith. My eyes filled with tears as he answered in the most beautiful, genuine, simplistic way. This was just another #butGod moment in our journey with Caleb.[1]

As a doer and a fixer, I wrestled hard with God during Caleb's recovery. Standing at the back of Caleb's room, listening to him knock every single answer out of the park, I realized just how wrong I had been to challenge God in this way. My idea of healing for Caleb had been getting him back to who he once was. In that moment, I realized just how much deeper God was working in Caleb. Every word came straight out of Caleb's heart. God was already using Caleb for His glory. I'm not sure it would have been the same had my prayers been answered the exact way I'd hoped.

EMILY'S JOURNAL AND OTHER UPDATES

March 26, 2018—Written in our home

I have often thought about the man who drove the semi-truck that hit Caleb and Clayton . . . Who is he? Where was he going? What did he see that night? How is he doing now?

The driver reached out to us on Friday through Facebook. We were able to schedule a phone call that took place this afternoon. It was so good to talk to him . . . to hear his perspective on the accident. We found out that after Caleb's truck skidded into his lane of traffic, it stopped completely right in front of him. When his semi hit on Caleb's side, it was with the force of about seventy-five thousand pounds. He could not believe that Caleb survived the impact and that he did not have a single broken bone. Neither can we!!! #butGod!

We were able to assure the driver that we hold no ill feelings toward him, and while we wish we could have met under different circumstances, we know there is a greater reason that he is in our lives. We ask you all to join us in praying for him as well.

On Saturday, before Caleb even knew that we would be talking to the driver of the semi, he said the following things:

"I want to talk to the truck driver, and tell him it's okay . . . it's not his fault."

"I hope he knows Jesus and if not that he gets saved."

Chapter 10

Preserved for a Purpose

YES AND YES AND YES: THE

ONLY FITTING RESPONSE

As weeks went by, Caleb made miraculous strides. Caleb was coming back to us, although so much was different. From his mannerisms to the cadence of his speech to his undying, awe-inspiring commitment to bring glory to God, it was as if Caleb was transformed. He was tenacious and doggedly committed to his therapy and the sometimes-painful daily exercises he needed to push through to regain independence. During this time, I found myself in a daily battle between staying positive and hiding my heartache. Before the accident, Caleb had finally earned so much of the independence teens strive for. Now he was fighting for the independence young children gain when they finally learn to walk, talk, and feed themselves. Regardless of the progress he was making, nearly everything he did required supervision.

With spring approaching, the month of May brought a sense of hope that we'd be leaving Craig with our son. Colorado was beautiful in the springtime—the mountains were still capped with snow, but the lower elevation was blanketed with lush grass and sweet-smelling flowers. That splendor felt like a gift from God. He would usher us out of Colorado with a goodbye replete with a fireworks display of bursting blooms.

When we finally left Craig, the goodbye was emotional

to say the least. How could we adequately thank a staff of people who had become like family and helped give us back someone we thought we'd lost forever? Emily, Caleb, and I did the rounds, thanking each and every staff member, often praying with them, of course, with tears in our eyes. Then came the packing. We had to pack up every single card Caleb had gotten in the mail, and there were thousands of them. It felt like packing boxes of blessings, sealing in the love God brought to us from around the world.

It had been our goal for Caleb to walk out of Craig on his own. Leaving became bittersweet because Caleb absolutely couldn't do this, but it was astounding enough that he could walk out with support from Emily and me. Although we felt some disappointment, we tried to focus our attention on the fact that Caleb could stand, which was a miracle on its own. As we walked toward the door, I strained to hold him up on the right side, and Emily did the same on the left side. Caleb's movements were still robotic and stiff, and he wore braces on his legs due to a tendon-lengthening surgery he underwent earlier that year. Had we let go, Caleb would have fallen.

With one of us on each side, supporting him with all our strength, Caleb slowly made his way toward the door. As we walked, people began to flood the lobby, cheering him on. People had come in on their day off, come in early, and made it a priority to see Caleb off. They had never done this before for a patient; the energy was thrilling and made us feel so loved. Emily and I could feel Caleb's momentum picking up as he took in the support. Suddenly it struck me as such a beautiful metaphor. Caleb had gotten through this with our support, and the doctors and therapists were behind us, but Caleb was leading the way.

It was the biggest moment since Caleb first nodded his head. "Walk outs" are now a tradition at Craig—one rooted in support for those who fight so hard for every single step.

Even after we said the last goodbye, gave the final hug, and completed our prayers, I knew there was one thank-you I wouldn't be able to adequately express until I was called home. Then I could thank Him for healing my son on earth.

———

Although we could have brought Caleb home when he was discharged, we had other plans. Doctors at Craig strongly recommended we look into a facility they often referred patients to. The facility, located in Nebraska, was called Quality Living, Inc. (QLI) and focused on helping people like Caleb learn how to live again without constant supervision or the persistent need for help with every small task. After five months, it was so tempting just to pack up and go home. I sometimes found myself daydreaming of family meals around the kitchen table. I missed goofing around with the kids in the living room, heading outside to play kickball, and just . . . being a normal family. When Emily and I prayed about QLI, however, there was no denying what God wanted us to do. He was gently nudging—then shoving—us toward the facility. It was something we couldn't ignore.

QLI was so much more than just another rehabilitation facility. The facility itself was made up of a series of houses, each with ten to twelve rooms that patients lived in. The rooms weren't like hospital rooms, which nearly every QLI resident had spent far too much time in already. Instead, the rooms were like small dorm rooms where residents were given the opportunity to take care of themselves. Caleb's home at QLI was also outfitted with a group kitchen and a living area, so he got to know the people living in the house with him. Caleb was the youngest. Of course, that didn't matter to him.

He'd become so outgoing—so gregarious—he would speak to anyone, making them laugh and making them think. Before the accident, Caleb had been shy, quiet, and reserved. Now he was social and silly, but he always kept one thing at the forefront of his mind no matter whom he interacted with: Jesus' love and His power to change lives. Seeing him minister to the folks at QLI—most of them twice, if not three times, his age—was such a beautiful thing, it made my heart thump hard in my chest and brought tears to my eyes. We continued to say #butGod.

During that time Emily and I slept in a little apartment nearby. We went straight to Caleb's place every morning. It was so cool going somewhere that, for the time being, belonged to Caleb. There were so many moments in the hospital, and even at Craig, when I wondered whether Caleb would remain in a state of infancy. Yet here he was, learning to put contacts in his eyes, feed himself, get around in his wheelchair, and more. But what makes QLI so spectacular is that they help the residents redefine their passions and explore their goals. Then they help them accomplish those goals one at a time. They taught Caleb to ride a bike again. They taught him how to kayak. They took him fishing. They made sure he could see a future worth living for, which, sadly, so many victims of tragic accidents never can imagine, let alone work toward.

In addition to learning how to participate in fun physical activities, Caleb began to show signs that his ever-growing devotion to God was becoming a huge part of his life. At QLI, God gave Caleb a heart for people and ministry. Sure, he was there to recover, but it was crystal clear that his true passions were getting to know other residents, encouraging them on their recovery journeys, and praying with them. Emily and I felt like we were watching the birth of Caleb's ministry because at QLI, he needed to be focused on himself, his own care, and his own support, but he put himself last. He only wanted to be an encouragement to others, make them laugh, and point them to Jesus. In his free time, Caleb would sit in the community room and read his Bible and listen to worship music. Anyone who came by was a person he could encourage in their healing—a soul Caleb could introduce to Jesus.

As Emily and I watched this unfold, we continued to see—without a shadow of a doubt—that God had kept

Caleb on this planet for a greater purpose. God's plan was not just to give him back to us, not just so we could enjoy our son again, but to accomplish real, eternal, spiritual things. Jesus modeled this when He said, "Not My will, but Yours, be done" (Luke 22:42 NKJV). Caleb became a shining example of that and had fully embraced the life God had given him. I, on the other hand, was still a work in progress.

Caleb's stay at QLI was completely transformative. Although he still struggled with his balance and had a tough time speaking clearly, seeing Caleb regain independence filled me with so much joy. It also slowly gave me back the faith that had faltered so dramatically following the accident. I no longer doubted God and was learning to forgive myself for doing so. Having had one son called home, it was nearly impossible to remain steadfast in my faith while watching Caleb remain unresponsive in a bed in the ICU for so many weeks. As a pastor, I initially found my wavering faith disorienting and scary. Since God created us, He knows how weak our humanity is, yet He remains faithful even when we are faithless. In our case, God took a tragedy and transformed it into an opportunity to minister in new and exciting ways—to glorify Him in every way possible.

After Caleb's two-month stay, leaving QLI was emotional. Caleb had made so many friends who loved him deeply, just as he loved them. Just like at Craig, Caleb walked around and said a personal goodbye to everyone he'd gotten to know. Although sadness comes with most good-byes, Caleb's parting gift to his new friends at QLI was the gift of renewed hope.

I wish I could say we went right home after this and began to adjust to our new normal as a family, but we had one more stop before taking Caleb home. One of the injuries Caleb sustained in the accident was a major wound to his left ear. We'd received advice from several surgeons that we should have Caleb's ear removed entirely and replaced with a prosthetic. However, Emily and I believed there had to be a better way.

Through a new friend who was following us on Facebook, in another #butGod moment, we were able to find a cele-brated pediatric facial reconstruction surgeon in Boise, Idaho. We sent him photos and set up a phone consultation. The doctor was convinced he could rebuild Caleb's ear, which we were so excited about. So, we went to Boise, and during a fourteen-hour surgery, the surgeon took pieces of Caleb's skin and bits of rib cartilage and rebuilt his ear. Thanks to this incredible surgeon, Caleb's left ear is a live, functioning ear with blood flow. We remained in Boise for one month while Caleb recovered. Then we finally went home for good with Caleb, our son whom I'd once known so well and now had the privilege of getting to know all over again.

EMILY'S JOURNAL AND OTHER UPDATES

From Caleb's dad

In the past six months, I've only spent a handful of days away from Caleb. We have always been close, but the bond we have now is stronger than ever. As I pull out of Omaha and head back home, I'm leaving a big part of my heart with Caleb, but I'm also taking a big part of my heart with me. I will miss Caleb so much, and I honestly don't know how I'll be away from him, but I am also ready to be with my other children and church family. What I know is, God's grace is sufficient.

Over the last six months, I've given everything I possibly have to Caleb. I've tried to be the best father, friend, caregiver, prayer warrior, encourager, and motivator I can. I've done everything I possibly can to help him and I'm driving away knowing that God's very best work in him is still to come. God's had this and God's got this!

Before I left, I was lying next to Caleb and we were talking. I was just looking at him and taking it all in before I left. Out of nowhere, Caleb said, "Dad, I think I want to recommit my life to Christ." I asked him why and he said, "Things just make more sense to me now and I want to make sure I'm following Christ fully." So . . . he prayed and asked God to use him and to help him follow Christ more wholeheartedly. It was so sweet and special . . . a great note for me to leave on!

Chapter 11

Surrender

MAY HIS WILL BE DONE

'll never forget the moment we walked back into our home in Oklahoma with Caleb. The house was the same—the boisterous laughter and joy of family; our familiar possessions; the smell of *us*—something you can only detect after time away. We were walking into that house the same but also forever changed. We had walked into this house broken after Trey stepped into heaven, and here we were again, trying to figure out what the next chapter looked like for us. Together we were wrecked, and now was the time to focus not only on Caleb's rehabilitation but also on our rehabilitation as a family. All we knew was #butGod.

Caleb was returning to our home a changed guy. I'm not just talking about his mannerisms, the cadence of his speech, or the added help he needed. All of those contributed to a feeling that we had to meet Caleb all over again. Our entire family unit had to get on the same page, welcoming Caleb into our hearts radically, passionately, completely. When we walked through the door with Caleb and came together in a family hug, we prayed and thanked God for His faithfulness and for being our anchor in a brutal storm. Caleb had been wrecked and made whole again, but he was also made different. He was left changed; he was rebuilt by God to honor Him and spread His glory here on earth.

As we settled Caleb back into the house, making sure

he had everything he needed to remain comfortable, he focused on keeping his room a sanctuary. It was a place where he could move freely, where he could worship actively one minute and study Scripture the next. After Emily and I had done our part of the work, we watched Caleb in his environment, becoming reacquainted with a "normal" teen's life. But Emily and I knew he was anything but normal.

During this time of adjustment, I couldn't help but remember Job. These words kept flowing through my mind: "I know that you can do all things, and that no purpose of yours can be thwarted" (Job 42:2). Job had lost everything he knew in the blink of an eye. He became the target of ridicule and judgment. Eventually, Job began demanding answers from the Lord. Why should God allow him to suffer when he was such a strong, fervent believer? Why should anyone who worshipped God so well suffer in this way?

Job knew he was indeed a sinner—not because of his actions, but because of who he was. For his entire life up to that point, Job had served the Lord, but only in prosperous circumstances. Now Job's faith was being truly tested. Job had no right to question God, His motives, or His purpose. Although it didn't happen overnight, Job began to recognize that God owed him nothing. As a result of his suffering, he developed a more intimate relationship with God and a better understanding of who God truly is. He ultimately was able to declare, "The LORD gave, and the LORD has taken away; Blessed be the name of the LORD" (1:21 NKJV).

Much like Caleb, and eventually our entire family, Job came to understand that God can and must be trusted in life, death, and everything in between. He alone would set His divine plan into motion and see it reach its full, intended purpose. As we often say in our home, "At the end of the day, either we trust God or we don't."

As we slowly transitioned into our new way of life, it became crystal clear that trauma and the resulting pain would either push us away from God or pull us toward God. Emily and I, along with our children, resolved to do the next right thing, one day at a time, knowing God would give us the strength for each day. Our children had endured the loss of Trey, had their lives turned upside down by Caleb's accident, and now were welcoming a new version of Caleb back into their lives. I secretly wondered whether they'd become bitter toward God, unable to trust Him through the suffering. That's the thing about pain though. It can make you resentful, screaming into the sky, "God, why? Just why?" or it can make you whisper, "Lord, we're going to trust You in it all because You are so good. You are worthy of our absolute trust." Thank goodness He is patient enough to wait for us to work through our torment and confusion. By God's grace, our family has been enveloped in the Lord's arms and has collectively grown stronger as a result of our suffering. Ultimately, we always come back to the same inevitable reality: Either we trust God or we don't. Our family has chosen to trust Him.

With each passing day, we have watched our children courageously accept and overcome the challenges we've all faced. I'm sure you have said to your kids or at least heard the phrase "God's plans are better than our dreams." We all have dreams of what we think should happen in our lives and in our kids' lives, and our kids hold some of those same hopes. But the Lord has His own plan. Our kids have surrendered to that as a part of this journey, and they have done so with such love and grace that I feel humbled by them daily.

Brittany is now a junior at Oklahoma Baptist University. She is a nursing major and wants to do medical missions. Clayton felt called to ministry and wants to be a pastor. Aubrey is strong and growing in her faith, and our little ones have remained resilient through it all as well. And Caleb feels so strongly called to ministry, his heart seems to lead him to shout his love of God from the mountaintops. I thank God for this because Caleb was about to find himself bringing people to Christ at a rate that would leave us all awestruck.

EMILY'S JOURNAL AND OTHER UPDATES

A text from Caleb

Everything I do comes from my purpose. So like the way I worship, the way I talk to people, the way I live my life all flow from the purpose God has given me and I've seen too many positive things come from it, so I owe it to Jesus to continue to move forward! I have the Spirit of the Lord upon me, once that is realized, anything is possible . . . God's given me a reason to live for Him. Jesus paid it all on the cross and that should cause us all to glory in Christ Jesus all our lives, but sometimes our flesh gets in the way and we lose sight of that. So God, being so good, gave us even another reason. He performed the miracle of saving Trey, so Trey is in heaven waiting for us. God knew this earth was going to be so hard on our family, so He brought Trey to Him so we can have extra motivation to get through this life. We should just live for Christ, but on days that are extra hard, we also do it for Trey.

Chapter 12

Called

WHEN MIRACLES LEAD TO MINISTRY

People toss around the word *miracle* all the time. They pull into Walmart, get a parking spot close to the store, and say, "Ah, it's a miracle."

Nope. Sorry, man. God did not move the earth to give you that parking spot. You just got lucky. A miracle is far bigger; it's when something unexplainable happens in the physical world. It is something supernatural and awe-inspiring.

As we began to see the new version of Caleb interacting with the world around him, the most breathtaking thing was watching how others responded to him with joy, compassion, and ultimately, open hearts. At Craig and QLI, the team only knew Caleb this way, yet we were seeing this changed person coming to life in the body of our once shy, reserved son. Never center stage, always in the background, Caleb had been the mischievous little guy who always got other people in trouble with smart maneuvers but wouldn't get into trouble himself. Unlike Brittany, who could be superdramatic; Clayton, who would barrel through the house like a freight train; Trey, who had an imagination that turned every couch in the house into a fort, boat, or cave; Aubrey, who was always giggling and dancing; or Luke and Addi with their endless energy, Caleb was our quiet guy, our shy guy, the most introspective of the bunch.

We were warned at Craig as Caleb began to come back to us that he might be different than he was before. We knew that was a risk because we'd seen it firsthand—people recovering from massive brain injuries who were unpredictable in a variety of ways. Some patients needed a security guard in their room at all times because they were a danger to themselves and others. They would get violent and strike out with their bare hands, cuss out their nurses, or throw things. Staff at Craig sometimes had to restrain them. Some patients were on suicide watch. Other people battled depression and had severe anxiety attacks. That's one of the worst parts of the recovery process: Some families are elated to have their loved one become conscious and communicative again, only to be slapped with the reality that their loved one really isn't coming back. Instead, the person is replaced with a new version of himself or herself—someone their families need protection from. Our family is so fortunate that although Caleb was different when he awoke, he was joyous, peaceful, and on fire for the Lord. That said, his faith is simple but deep. The religious façade he once knew is gone. It's all about a real, personal relationship with God.

As I look back, I am able to see this thread so clearly. As Caleb came back to us, his first prayers were that God would allow him to run again. However, over time, these prayers changed to "God, use my life in whatever way You want for Your glory." He was indeed running, but he was running a different race. What an incredible shift for a young man to make in the midst of what many would view as a never-ending tragedy. To the contrary, Caleb likes to say that the brain injury is a gift from God. Caleb believes God gifted him with the injury to remind him that he shouldn't be here on earth; because he was spared by God, and because of his disabilities, he is dependent on God every day to make it through. God uses him exactly as he is.

The apostle Paul wrote, "Blessed be the God and Father of our Lord Jesus Christ, the Father of mercies and God of all comfort, who comforts us in our affliction" (2 Cor. 1:3–4). I love that scripture because essentially God is saying, "You need to come to Me, the God of comfort, because you are going to have pain. You are going to need comfort in this fallen world. Let Me comfort you. Let Me help you. Let Me lead you." As a family, we have learned that the God of comfort, who comforts us in our pain, uses us to comfort others.

It was at QLI that Caleb really began to have a heart for people and wanted to minister to them. Once that passion for ministry took hold, he was unstoppable. He was compelled to be an evangelist, pointing people to Christ and encouraging them on their journey to knowing God intimately. Man, did he ever.

After we were home getting Caleb settled, we immediately saw this sharp shift toward ministry. Previously shy Caleb, who would rather do anything than talk to a stranger, suddenly never went anywhere without talking to at least one new person—usually many, many more. A simple grocery run could take three hours while Caleb walked the aisles stopping every person he saw, bringing them joy, learning about them, and offering prayers. Sure, there were times I wanted to get home with a jug of milk that was still cold, but I couldn't help but continue watching in awe as my son proved to me that God had redeemed what we thought was lost. Caleb taught me to be in the moment every day and to remain present, even with complete strangers.

In August 2018, Caleb went back to school, and he was a man on a mission. Having had so much practice talking to new people, he saw that his purpose was to make a difference. On Caleb's first day back, the entire student body came out to welcome him. The marching band played, his teammates and coaches were present, and his friends were right by his side. As we got out of the car, the high school principal asked if Caleb would offer a prayer—at a public school. Caleb's speech was still very slurred then, and I was nervous for him. But he stood up with a walker's assistance and offered the most beautiful, heartfelt, gospel-centered prayer. I remember thinking, *This is now his mission field, and God is going to use him mightily.* From that day forward Caleb wanted to meet everybody in the school and learn all their names before he graduated. He had two years to do that, and though the COVID-19 pandemic cut things short, he learned so many people's names that Caleb became the most popular person in the school. Caleb liked to say, "Everyone knows my name, but I want them to know they are more important than me, so I want to learn their names."

He had some incredible experiences his last two years of high school: he was able to run a 5K with his cross-country team; he won homecoming king his senior year; and he was able to make the first basket on senior night with his varsity basketball team. Instead of letting these moments inflate his ego, Caleb saw each as a platform for bringing people to Jesus. He never wasted or made one moment about himself. It was always about making his accomplishments reflect Jesus.

We laugh and say that the new Caleb would annoy the old Caleb. It's true. The new Caleb would drive the old Caleb crazy. However, there's no denying the new Caleb is driving more people to real, deep, purposeful faith than we ever could have dreamed. Watching him truly live his life for the glory of God is one of the most beautiful things I have ever seen. #butGod.

EMILY'S JOURNAL AND OTHER UPDATES

A text from Caleb

Don't let the world tell you that it's okay to lose your fire for Jesus BC it seems many other Christians do at some point! You wanna know how I will NEVER lose my fire! BC EVERY SINGLE morning I wake up to the same old nightmare that I used to have that has now become a reality! I can't run, can't play sports, can't talk normal . . . I run into things, fall down (and have the stitches to prove it) . . . so I wonder why God would allow this? But that's when God quickly hits me with the reality that my struggles are just reminders of how much I need Him and how much better life is with Him. What would be better: to go to hell with a perfectly healthy body, or to go to heaven with a brain injury? I choose the brain injury. God has totally changed my life and I will forever live on fire for Jesus and consider my brain injury the best gift I could ever receive because God has used it to bring me to Him. Just pray I don't waste one second. I love you so much dad.

Chapter 13

Impact-Hungry

WHERE ABUNDANCE ALWAYS LEADS

W ithin the first few weeks of being home in Oklahoma, Caleb and I started getting invitations to speak at conferences, events, and church gatherings. Although Caleb was still recovering, performing daily exercises to promote rehabilitation, he was ready to hit the road and fulfill his mission to deliver God's message on an even larger scale. It didn't take long for me to realize that God was doing something huge through Caleb. I was just grateful to get a front-row seat and be along for the ride.

The first big event we were invited to was a gathering in Tulsa at Oral Roberts University. The meeting would be held at the Mabee Center, where the school's team played basketball games. It was not your regular gym—more like a stadium with seats cascading from the ceiling. This awesome venue was rented out by an Oklahoma megachurch for a youth event that would host two thousand kids, ages twelve through eighteen. On our way to the event that morning was the first time Caleb rocked out in my truck to worship music, banging his head to the beat, raising his hands in reverence, and trying to match his slurred words to the lyrics. I wasn't used to this new side of Caleb, who never sang out loud before the accident. I wouldn't say it made me uncomfortable, but I was unclear about whether or not I should participate—so I zoned out on the road, letting Caleb do his thing, glancing at him every so often and smiling.

———

After a while, Caleb lowered the music and took a break from worship. During this time, I figured I'd ask Caleb what he thought about what we should say. Yes, you read that correctly: We hadn't planned our speech. Caleb glanced over at me and simply said, "Dad, you just take the lead and I'll follow."

My pastor brain went into overdrive trying to remember a sermon—any sermon—I'd delivered that could fit the situation and speak to the young demographic. My mind was blank and my heart began to race, but as soon as we arrived at the venue and walked inside, peace washed over me. I knew God was there with us, and He would deliver His perfect message through Caleb, who had practiced ministering to every person we'd encountered for the past year. Caleb had this because God had Caleb. I was there to honor God and support my son.

As the Lord led me and I ushered Caleb, our flow was incredible. Caleb was sincere, engaging, and so funny. Before the talk at the Mabee Center, we'd been invited to speak at a Bible study for women. I was comfortable with that one because there were a lot of moms and older ladies whom I knew would be forgiving if Caleb was goofy or said something off-color. And my goodness, did he ever. One of the first things I asked him onstage was, "How are you feeling today?"

Caleb responded, "Well, I'm really good with older women, so I'm doing great!"

That was the moment I realized Caleb had a gift onstage. He was able to expertly toe the line between humor, innocent irreverence, and humble endearment. He had his audience completely captivated without even trying. This was the same shy kid who would have never spoken to any audience prior to the wreck. God had totally transformed Caleb from the inside out.

That day at ORU, we got up and spoke and lots of people came forward to give their lives to Christ. In fact, an entire basketball team from Stillwater, Oklahoma, came forward. I will never forget it. They came down front where Caleb was standing, all looking at him with eyes of wonder. It was as if they knew they were looking at a miracle and God had used Caleb to bring these guys to faith in Jesus. One by one, Caleb gave a fist bump to each person who had received Christ, making such a personal and meaningful connection. I remember that night driving home from Tulsa thinking, *Okay, God is doing something more than I could have ever imagined.* That was the beginning of the #butGod movement, catalyzed through Caleb.

In February 2020, one month before the pandemic, we were invited out to a little town in Oklahoma to speak at a Fellowship of Christian Athletes event. When we made our final arrival arrangements, the organizer told me that Caleb and I should meet her by the cafeteria. That day when we pulled into the school, I wasn't able to find the cafeteria, but I saw a gymnasium with a nearly empty parking lot and decided to pull in there.

Right as I put the car in park, a young lady came walking out of the gym in her basketball uniform. Assuming she was a basketball player, I rolled down my window and said, "Hey, can you tell me where the cafeteria is?"

She started to give me directions, but her mom pulled up before she was able to finish telling me where to go. Her mom rolled down her window, and her daughter climbed into the front seat. She nodded at her daughter and called out to me, "Hey, just follow us and we'll show you where it is!"

I pulled out of the spot and followed them, weaving around the school. As the woman slowed down, I pulled into a spot, got out of the car, and turned my back to go around and help Caleb. The mom and daughter got out of their car and walked over to us. The mom said, "Oh my goodness! Are you Caleb Freeman?"

"Yes, ma'am!" Caleb replied.

"Oh, I saw that you were going to be in town tonight. I wish we could come hear you speak. Unfortunately, we won't be able to be there," she said, tilting her head.

Not one to take no for an answer, Caleb started laying it on thick. "What's more important than coming tonight? I bet you can make it happen! I believe in you and believe you are supposed to come." At this point, Caleb began begging with wide eyes and a huge, sweet smile. "Come on, you need to be there! I may never be back in this town again."

Finally, the woman gave in and said with a chuckle, "Okay, we'll try."

We said our goodbyes and walked toward the building. I was absolutely certain they wouldn't be coming that night.

A couple of hours later, we were ushered back to the gym where the event was about to begin. To my amazement, the very last two people to walk in were the mom and her daughter. Apparently they decided to come after all. Yep, I know. Caleb's good. Caleb flashed them his crooked million-dollar smile. I waved to them just before Caleb and I walked to the middle of the basketball court and launched into our talk. Although there were between three and four hundred people in the audience, right in front of me at midcourt sat this mom and daughter. I looked at them the whole night as if we were speaking only to them. We shared Caleb's story, and when we got to the very end—as I always did to wrap things up—I gave everybody an opportunity to give their lives to Christ. I walked back and forth, presented the gospel, and explained how to repent of sins, trust in Jesus, and submit to Him as Lord. Finally I said, "If you would like to do this, pray with me."

The room was silent.

After the prayer, I said, "If you just prayed that prayer, please raise your hand."

The very first hand that went up was the daughter's. With tears in her eyes and a wide smile on her face, she gave her life to Christ that night.

As Caleb and I headed home in the dark, passing vehicles on the highway sent flashes of light bursting through the car. As I gazed at the road I said to Caleb, "Do you realize had you not had your brain injury, we would never have been in that town tonight? Or maybe ever. What are the odds of us pulling into the gym at the very moment that young lady was walking out? What are the odds of her mom recognizing you? What are the odds of you begging them to come back, and *because* of them coming back, that girl giving her life to the Lord?"

As we drove, a phrase kept pressing into my heart: *God is not in the odds. He is above them*. Caleb says it best: "God's favorite hobby is beating the odds."

It began to dawn on me that I had such a tight grip on things in my life—including the steering wheel in that moment. I had a tight grip on my family, a tight grip on my ministry, a tight grip on my goals. Instead of accepting this about me, God had to peel back my fingers, one by one, so I could live with an open hand and not a closed one. I had to be willing to loosen my grip on all things and surrender completely. We don't get to say, "God, You get 90 percent of my life, but I'm keeping 10 percent for me."

Instead, God says you release it all to Him. Trusting Him can be the hardest thing to do, right? The very first commandment is, "You shall have no other gods before Me" (Ex. 20:3 NKJV). God doesn't say that He wants to be the best of many gods in your life. He wants to be the *only* God. It would be like me telling my wife, "Emily, I love you more than all the other women I love in my life." That does not mean anything to her.

She would say, "I don't want to share your love with other women; I want you to love me and only me." That's the essence of what it means to worship God.

What happened to Caleb on December 19, 2017, was no accident, nor was anything that happened afterward—including this girl who came to Christ. God arranged that. I could tell a hundred stories similar to this one. It continues to be the essence of what God is doing with Caleb's journey. I had to come to grips with the fact that God's plans are way better than my dreams. It's just the plain and simple truth. I begged God to give me cancer and let Trey live. I begged for that exchange and spent many hours bargaining with God for his life. I had many dreams for Caleb too; I wanted Caleb to be a starter on the basketball team and I wanted him to get a scholarship and run cross-country in college. Parents can identify with these kinds of aspirations. Yet, as hard as I prayed, God pried this out of my hands. I had the death grip on my dreams for my kids, but God spoke to me words that were both comforting and nearly impossible to swallow: "Jeremy, I love your children. I love them more than you do."

God has shown this truth in all our children—Brittany, Clayton, Trey, Aubrey, Luke, Addi, and Caleb. And though Caleb has seemingly lost the most here on earth, what he has gained makes the losses pale in comparison. Watching Caleb struggle has been heartbreaking at times, but I have learned to accept that everything—even the gut-wrenching things—has a purpose that is beyond what we can fathom. For instance, the Lord allowed death into our life through a child. We did not ask for that. We would not want that. If we could choose it, we would never choose it, but that's what God allowed. Through this, I learned that I can either be resentful because of my suffering, or I can be faithful through it by allowing Him to use it all for His glory. Man, is that hard when He chooses to take one of your children—to allow such tragedy and heartache. I try to remember that one day I will be with Trey again in heaven for ten million-plus years, and during that time, this life will feel like a breath—light and momentary. We have to live with eternal perspective, because if we don't, then we will never do anything that really matters.

From the get-go, once he was conscious and able to communicate again, it became clear that Caleb has that eternal perspective. He sees the unseen.

While we were heavily involved in speaking gigs, we were also receiving dozens of prayer requests each week and opportunities to minister to others going through hard things. One particular note we received was about a young lady, engaged to be married, who got in a car wreck on her way back from college. She didn't suffer a brain injury, but she did suffer a spinal injury. Caleb and I talked it over and felt nervous about going to pray for her because we knew the odds were stacked against her—I mean *really* stacked against her. She was in the ICU at OU Health, and after debating it for some time, Caleb felt compelled to go and pray for her. I hopped on board immediately.

When we got to the hospital, the family told us the chances of her walking again were nearly zero, but that didn't deter us. I looked at the family and said, "The odds were stacked against Caleb too. I don't know what God's will is. God's will may be that she is in a wheelchair for the rest of her life, or He may heal her. We are going to ask Him to heal her."

We prayed for her, believing God could heal her. We were thrilled to discover this was one of the times the Lord chose to heal here on earth. This girl was never supposed to walk again, but slowly, she began to make progress that was nothing short of miraculous. Following her time in the ICU, she went to Craig Hospital and eventually regained her ability to walk. She got married a year later and is doing extremely well. This, after she was told there was little to no hope. Yet, Caleb, relentless in his pursuit for God's glory, refused to believe healing was not a possibility. Sometimes healing takes nothing more than faith and trust in Him and the willingness and confidence to act on it.

But God doesn't always choose the miracle you envision, even if every decision He makes is ultimately for our good and His glory. Not long after we met with the victim of the spinal injury, we felt strongly that we needed to minister to another young lady in Oklahoma. She had been in a car accident a year before Caleb and had not made any progress for five years, but we felt compelled to visit. Caleb and I went to pray for her, and about a month later, God called her home. She died from pneumonia. Her mom called us and said that the fact that we came and ministered to them meant so very much to their family. The outcomes are not always what we want, but obedience is the goal. It's not the outcome, but the obedience; and when you obey God, you entrust the outcomes to Him, even if they threaten to ruin you when they come to fruition. Caleb and I will never stop opening our hearts to God, listening, and ministering to those in the darkest of hours. We know the truth about being wrecked: Brokenness often invites the miraculous. This is something we are called to embrace. All God asks is for us to be faithful.

Although we might want to, we don't control God. We would like to tell God what to do, or even play God at times. But honestly, if we were truthful about it, we really don't want to be God because He knows the whole story from beginning to the end. Although we are the ones who think we know what is best, we can never know without the infinite, eternal knowledge that belongs to God alone.

I really struggled with this notion when Trey was sick. What if God were to heal Trey? Let's say that Trey lived a normal, healthy life but never trusted God. What if he was able to run and jump and do all the things you want your kids to be able to do in life, but then what if he died without Christ? If Boss Day never happened, Trey's future after death would have been uncertain. That was a hard lesson to learn: A person's greatest need is not physical healing but spiritual healing. We obviously want both, and Christians ultimately get both in heaven, but on earth we don't always get the physical healing we desire. Caleb's greatest need was not to be healed from his brain injury, but to be forgiven of his sins and become God's relentless ambassador.

I am going to live the rest of my life here, until I get to heaven, with a certain hole in my heart. My heart is not perfectly whole because I miss my son Trey so very much and still mourn the losses of my children's healthy, physical bodies now and again. But I try not to let my pain define me. Instead, I want God to use my pain as a reminder and a motivator. A reminder that this world is not our home, and a motivator to live each day as if it could be our last to advance the gospel. God alone can bring purpose to our pain.

Our role in the big picture, as God unfolds His will for our lives, is to go to the hard place where Jesus went. When Jesus was praying in the garden of Gethsemane, he poured out His heart. Jesus said, "If it is possible, let this cup pass from Me" (Matt. 26:39 NKJV). What was the cup? It was the cup of suffering. He was essentially saying, "If there be any other way, let this suffering pass from Me. Yet, not My will, but *Your will* be done." I think you finally know you are where God wants you to be in life when you can genuinely say, "God, I want *Your* will to be done." That is a hard place to get to because God's will is often different from what we would want or choose, but His will is always best.

EMILY'S JOURNAL AND OTHER UPDATES

From Caleb's Dad

God gave me 2 Corinthians 4:18 when I was a senior in high school. Little did I know at that time, it would be such a powerful truth I would refer back to so many times in my life. What is the verse, you ask?

"So we fix our eyes not on what is seen, but on what is unseen, since what is seen is temporary, but what is unseen is eternal" (NIV).

Over the years, a phrase emerged in my heart from this verse reflecting what this scripture meant to me. It was: "Living with an eternal perspective." For all of my Christian life, I have tried to live with eternity at the front of my heart and mind.

My wife wrote a beautiful reflection about perspective in a prayer she prayed for Caleb early on:

> When Jalinda (the lady who showed up on the scene of the accident) told us that she prayed over Caleb from the top of his head to the bottom of his feet I also started to pray for Caleb in this way.
>
> Heavenly Father, I pray for Caleb's head. Only You can see what is going on in that head. I ask that all of the neurons will reconnect, and that the cells would function fully and miraculously. Most of all that he would have the mind of Christ, that his mind

would be renewed day by day, and that his thoughts would be pleasing to You. Fill his mind with Your truth continually.

I pray for Caleb's ear. As his ear is healing, I pray that it will serve as a reminder of the accident and a reminder of God's faithfulness each day. The ear will become a spiritual marker to set Caleb apart as He listens to Your voice and obeys. Please give him ears to hear and perfectly understand what Your purpose is for his life.

I pray for Caleb's eyes. His physical eyesight has always struggled and he requires glasses to see clearly. As he wakes up I ask that You allow him to see clearly the things that really matter. That he will see people with Your eyes so that he can love them with Your love.

I pray for Caleb's mouth. May he be able to speak clearly and boldly about the hope of Jesus Christ and the Spirit of God inside of him. May the words of his mouth be pleasing in Your sight. May laughter fill his mouth once again. And may praise be always on his lips as he declares all that You have done for him.

I pray for Caleb's heart. Make him a man after Your own heart. Let him love the Lord with all of his heart, soul, mind, and strength. Let his heart beat in rhythm with Your Spirit. Give him a healthy heartbeat and give him a heart of endurance.

I pray for Caleb's lungs. That they will remain clear and strong. I pray that as Caleb inhales, he will inhale Your grace, and as he exhales, he will exhale Your praise.

For Caleb's body to be fully restored, for his arms to be strong and fluid in motion, for his legs to regain what they have lost and carry him swiftly once again. For him to walk in Your ways and follow the path that You have for him. For his center to be You and You alone.

For him to know You and to make You known all his days on this earth. To be Your instrument, Your mouthpiece, and Your disciple.

In Jesus' name,

Amen

Chapter 14

Never Give Up,
Never Give In,
Never Let Go

MANTRA OF A MAN OF GOD

Cross-country runners need an internal motor because there are parts of the course where nobody is there to cheer you on. Nobody can see you, so you've got to cheer yourself on. You've got to push hard from deep within. Caleb possessed this never-give-up, never-give-in, never-let-go attitude before the wreck. And the wreck did not change that. He is more expressive now, but he always had a God-given inner strength that was absolutely beautiful to witness. Everyone has been able to see that on full display in his life since the accident. A brain injury is a long-distance run, and Caleb is the best long-distance runner I know. I wouldn't want anybody else running in that spot. He is the one who can get it done one step at a time.

One of our dear friends posted some incredible words about Caleb, and she associated cross-country running with Caleb's injury. Her son and Caleb ran cross-country together at the high school. Before the accident, Caleb was the heart and soul of the cross-country team. He was a quiet leader that everybody looked to. Running was so effortless for him. Boy, I miss watching that boy run. He had a pure and naturally competitive spirit, but he was not your rah-rah guy. He didn't run around chest bumping guys and high-fiving. He would go out to the middle of a field and kneel down to pray, and when he came back, he would take off and never look back. That's kind of how he has handled this brain injury too.

Emily's aunt was a great gift to us because she would come up to the ICU and stay with Caleb right after the wreck. I never wanted to leave him, and I didn't want to sleep. She would come up and stand by Caleb and say, "Jeremy, you rest. I'm just going to watch him." She would stand over Caleb and allow me to sleep, which was such a blessing. She was the one who began to say early on, "Caleb, never give up, never give in, never let go. You are going to have to fight. You have to develop a never-give-up attitude. You have to press on. You have to endure."

Somewhere along this journey, Caleb latched on to that idea. It became his mantra: Never give up, never give in, never let go. In other words, he embodied this grit, this determination to not only get better but also to not waste a moment. This has become our family theme. We will get through whatever this earthly life hands us. We will overcome it because God has seen us through so much, and we've learned we can trust Him.

I specifically remember a verse that became important when Caleb was in the hospital. Numbers 14:24 says, "Because my servant Caleb has a different spirit and follows me wholeheartedly, I will bring him into the land he went to, and his descendants will inherit it" (NIV). One of the things we prayed for Caleb was that when he woke up, he would have a different spirit, and he really does. God answered that prayer.

Caleb woke up in more ways than one, you could say. Caleb actually believes—and we've had to walk through this with him very carefully—that he began to genuinely follow Jesus *after* the accident, not before. He made the decision to follow Jesus as a child, but he wasn't actively walking with God before the wreck. Caleb likes to say the wreck didn't turn his life upside down; the wreck turned his life in the right direction. I ended up baptizing Caleb again a year after the wreck because he really did believe that he genuinely trusted in Christ after the accident. The Bible teaches that baptism follows salvation, so we wanted to get Caleb's baptism on the right side of his salvation. All I can say about that is he has been transformed by Jesus Christ, 100 percent. Being a Christian is not about going from bad to good. It is about going from being dead to being alive. God used the near-death experience to awaken Caleb to life spiritually.

In every Christian's life suffering is certain. The apostle Peter wrote, "Do not be surprised at the fiery trial when it comes upon you to test you, as though something strange were happening to you. But rejoice insofar as you share Christ's sufferings, that you may also rejoice and be glad when his glory is revealed" (1 Peter 4:12–13). We don't like to talk about it because it's hard and painful, but suffering is inevitable. In a fallen world, things happen that we don't enjoy because we are living under the curse of sin. That means there will be death, sickness, disease, natural disaster, all the brokenness of the world, and the brokenness of our lives, but pain reminds us that we are not meant to live here forever. Every heartache and all suffering remind us that we are not home yet.

C. S. Lewis said, "God whispers to us in our pleasures, speaks in our conscience, but shouts in our pains: it is His megaphone to rouse a deaf world."[1] I think suffering is what God uses to honestly and most often bring Himself glory because true followers of Jesus will follow Jesus regardless of the suffering. They are going to endure. They are going to persevere.

Do you know who Joni Eareckson Tada is? She is a hero. I don't know her personally. I've never met her. But she is a hero to me and so many others. She was paralyzed from the neck down when she was seventeen years old, and for the past forty years, she has lived as a paraplegic. She has had cancer twice. She has lived and continues to live an extremely hard life. A few years ago I heard Joni Eareckson Tada speak at a conference, and her message still encourages me through suffering. She was asked about what she'll do in heaven with glorified legs. She talked about how the first thing she'll do is fall to her knees in gratitude and how God uses our suffering to make us more like Jesus. How could we resent something—like a car accident, paralysis, cancer—that makes us more like Jesus? She answered as if she'd thought about this a million times. She looked so confident in knowing exactly what she'll do first when she gets to heaven.[2]

God has used suffering in my life to shift my focus toward what is most important. As a parent, you have these dreams for your kids. You want to watch them play sports or excel at whatever they are doing and enjoy that, but what happens when that is taken away from you, when your kid can't do what you want them to do? You discover the "little gods" in your life. Emily and I were athletes. I had all these great aspirations to watch our kids play sports and do well. All of that was taken from me—all of it. And guess what? At the end of the day, does that even really matter? You want it to matter, but it doesn't. God has a way of stripping away the things to which you so tightly cling and actually freeing you to live in a meaningful way, and that pretty much sums up our life. As my friend Randy Alcorn says, "Let what will matter to you five minutes after you die, matter the most right now."[3]

Caleb walked in the house last night with a big bruise on his nose. I said, "Caleb, what did you do?"

"Uh . . ." He doesn't like to tell us when he falls. Finally, he confessed that he was in his room with his eyes closed, and when he turned and kneeled down, he hit his face on a box fan he has. He did it while worshipping, which is pretty funny.

"Caleb," I said, "just open your eyes and look around before you kneel down." He is so *all-in* that he doesn't even think about that. I miss watching my son walk into a room without bumping into something. I miss being able to go outside and shoot baskets with him. I miss hearing him talk without struggling. On the days when I'm not walking in the Spirit and I'm walking in the flesh, I can get in a kind of negative space. I hate that sometimes I have to hold Caleb as he walks up and down stairs. Those are just little things. I hate that he can't get in his car and drive down the road. I worry about him getting married. Is he going to find somebody who wants to live with him in an understanding way? These are all things that concern me. Those things are of no concern to Caleb because he has learned how to be content in all circumstances. As he likes to say, "It's a snare to compare."

A few months after Caleb returned home, he was feeling a little discouraged. My wife encouraged him to begin memorizing more Scripture. Caleb, not one to do things half-hearted, memorized the entire book of Philippians. Keep in mind, his doctors said he would struggle with short-term memory loss, so to memorize and retain an entire book of the Bible is #butGod. As Caleb filled his mind with truth, that truth transformed his outlook on life, and he knows that "He who began a good work in him, will be faithful to complete it at the day of Christ Jesus" (Phil. 1:6, paraphrased).

John 11:35 is the shortest verse in the Bible: "Jesus wept." Have you stopped and thought about *why* he wept? He was about to do this incredible miracle, to raise Lazarus from the dead, yet He wept alongside the mourners grieving Lazarus.

Why would Jesus weep when He was about to do something so awesome? Why didn't He look at all these people and say, "What's wrong with you? I'm about to raise Lazarus from the dead. Stop your crying!"

Instead of doing that, He wept with them. Why? Because this action gives us a glimpse into the heart of God. God takes no pleasure in our pain, nor is He separate from our pain. God is not the cosmic killjoy. God is not up in heaven trying to ruin things or force us to live miserable lives. No. He weeps with us. He feels pain with us. He is with us.

You might say, "Well, if God is so good and God is so loving, why doesn't He stop weeping with us and do something about our pain?"

Here is what I say to people who think this way: God *did* do something about our pain. He came to earth, lived in the flesh, died on the cross, and rose again so our pain doesn't have the final say. God has the final say. That is what #butGod is all about. Yes, we live with pain; that's a natural part of this life. But God comforts us, strengthens us, and one day in eternity will completely free us of all pain. That's the beautiful hope of the gospel.

When I hear anyone questioning God's actions (or perhaps what they qualify as inactions), what I hear is them suggesting God doesn't really care about us. Why would a loving God allow pain into our lives? Here is my perspective on that. Let's say you don't believe in God. Does cancer still happen? Yep. Does death still happen? Yeah. Even if you don't believe in God, all those things still happen. The question is: Do you want to handle all of that on your own, or do you want to go through that awful experience with Someone by your side, holding you up, giving your suffering even greater purpose?

I think you would much rather say, "Man, I actually believe there is a God who created a perfect world. Sin wrecked it, and because of sin, brokenness abounds. But because God is so good, He has not left us on our own. He remains with us at all times, and not just when things are good. He comes to us in our own brokenness. He sometimes heals our pain temporarily on this earth, but even when He doesn't, He gives us what we need to endure. One day though, He will heal us completely forever in heaven."

Without a belief in God, there is no beauty in the story of life, nor is there a point to suffering. Without God, you believe your pain is all there is and healing is only possible through beating the odds on your own. Instead of dreaming of redemption, you picture dying and going into the ground. That's it. There's nothing more to it. If you ask me, that's a horrible way to live. And I find most people don't necessarily live like this when things are good. Yet, we can't blame God when things go badly and take the credit when things go well.

Ask yourself the bigger questions in life and be honest about the answers. God brings purpose to your pain and suffering. Caleb's life is a perfect example of pain redeemed.

Remember the words of the apostle Paul as he shared the secret of contentment:

> For I have learned in whatever situation I am to be content. I know how to be brought low, and I know how to abound. In any and every circumstance, I have learned the secret of facing plenty and hunger, abundance and need. I can do all things through him who strengthens me. (Phil. 4:11–13)

Believe me, Christ strengthens you—but not through experiences you will necessarily welcome or love. Sometimes He wrecks you to remind you of His infinite love, and that only in and through Him will you be completely satisfied.

EMILY'S JOURNAL AND OTHER UPDATES

From Caleb's Dad

The word *posture* means disposition or one's state of being. I love this word. I often ask myself, *What is the posture of my heart or my most consistent disposition?* Truly, I think our posture says much. Caleb's physical posture is not great. He struggles. He walks off-balance, leans to the right, and still stumbles quite often. I find myself getting frustrated with this at times. Not frustrated at Caleb but at the fact that doing simple things is so hard for him. But Caleb has a great posture—a better posture—and it is the posture of his heart. If I had to classify the posture of Caleb's heart in one word, I would say that word is *worship.* Caleb loves, absolutely loves, to worship God. He does it primarily by reading God's Word, singing, praying, and sharing Jesus. Truly his heart is worship and because of that he cannot help himself when he hears worship music. He generally just lifts his hands, falls to his knees, or gets on his face before God! Many Sundays I look over and Caleb is lying face down in the middle of the worship service. It doesn't matter that he's in a room full of people or that he's the only one in that position. It's just him and his Savior, and he is fully abandoned and caught up in His glory.

It's so amazingly genuine, very moving, and very convicting.

Caleb is the most pure and genuine person I know. He

truly believes his purpose on earth is to encourage people, make them smile, and tell them about Jesus. So simple, yet so profound!

Our inward posture always impacts our outward posture, and because Caleb's heart is so genuinely connected to God's heart, it's evident in everything he does. Yes, he walks with a limp; that's his natural, physical posture that is reflective of his brain. *But* his spiritual posture in worship is reflective of his heart that loves His Savior so much.

Epilogue

About a year and a half after Caleb's accident, I went on a mission trip to Mozambique, Africa, and I experienced a moment with God that radically changed my life. Until that point I had felt like I was living life with a cloud over my head. Even the brightest moments, including Caleb's miraculous healing, were still covered with this cloud.

On September 1, 2013, I watched my son Trey take his final breath. It was the most difficult day of my life, and when Trey stepped into heaven, a part of me died. I knew that was a part I wouldn't fully get back until I got to heaven myself, so I began living with a bit of a "death complex." With all the heartache my family and I had suffered, I had found myself merely existing, instead of living the abundant life God had for me.

Something changed in me on my trip to Africa though. One night as we were beginning our worship service, several of the African pastors got on stage and began dancing. These were pastors who lived in an area that was recently devastated by a cyclone. Many of them lost their homes, churches, friends, and family members, but their losses didn't keep them from celebrating. I watched them sing and worship the Lord with sincere gladness, and as I watched these pastors and their wives, I got teary-eyed. I began repeating to myself, "I want to live." I said it again and again and again, "I want to live!" Something happened in my heart that I hadn't felt in a long time: I wanted to live. That may not seem like a big deal, but I couldn't remember the last time I had felt that way. As I declared I wanted to live, the cloud lifted, and I felt the "Son" shining on me. As Trey used to say, "I was crying happy tears."

In an instant, God changed my perspective. He had lifted the cloud. I finally wanted to embrace and enjoy the life God had given me. I wanted to relish the time with my wife and children. I wanted to enjoy leading my church. I wanted to enjoy time with my friends. I wanted to enjoy watching my kids play and grow. I wanted to enjoy getting up each day.

I will always terribly miss Trey, and I will miss watching Caleb do things he was able to do before his accident, but I am no longer letting those losses cause me to miss the other things right in front of me. Enjoying my life didn't mean I loved Trey any less. I love him with all my heart. The mere thought of him brings me smiles and tears. But I have to live or else I'll be miserable. I can honestly say, "I want to live." That doesn't mean I'm not ready for heaven or eager for the Lord's return, because I am. It just means that until Jesus returns or calls me home, I'm going to take the life God has given me and live it. This earth is not my home, and I am just passing through. But as I do, I will live this life with joy and for the glory of God, just like Caleb. God is with me; He has never and will never leave me.

God has been so good to us. He has met us every step of the way and continues to carry us. He has helped me declare "I want to live," and He continues to teach me how to do that. It is a choice every single day. Obedience is a choice. Even though it would be "easier" to have Trey back with us and for Caleb to not have a brain injury, it is simply not the life God has given us. Easier is not always better. God has allowed hard things, and we have to trust Him with what He has allowed. Doing so isn't easy either. In fact, anyone who has genuinely tried to obey God knows how hard it is. Emily and I learned a long time ago not to compare lives. Someone always has it easier, and someone always has it harder. Each of us is simply called to live the life God gives us and trust Him no matter what.

So, here we are in our midforties, living with loss, raising little ones again, navigating the challenges of brain injury, trying to figure out Caleb's future, trusting God with so many things with our other kids, trying to pastor and lead our church well, and on and on. But above all, we just keep seeking to obey God one day at a time! We cling daily to this truth from Philippians 1:6 that says, "And I am sure of this, that he who began a good work in you will bring it to completion at the day of Jesus Christ." And we continue to live with this prayer and hope: "I want you to know, brothers, that what has happened to me has really served to advance the gospel" (Phil. 1:12).

This is our #butGod story. What is your story? If you do not have a #butGod story, we would love to share with you the hope we have in Jesus and the hope you can have in Him too. If our story has encouraged you in some way, we would love to hear that as well. If you need prayer, we would love to pray for you. If you would like Caleb to come and share at your church, school, business, or organization, you can reach us at hashtagbutGod@gmail.com.

What's next for Caleb and our family? Only God knows. He has written our story from beginning to end, and we are just trying to walk in it with faith. I know God will do whatever will be for our good and His glory. And to that, I say, "Yes and amen." Please continue to pray for Caleb and our family. We are nobodies, trying to tell everybody, all about Somebody who changed our lives.

#butGod . . .

Acknowledgments

This book would not exist without the countless people who have poured into my life and the life of my family. It's hard to narrow a list, but as I reflect on this book, I am indebted to the following people:

My wife, Emily. There are no words to describe how much you mean to me. Next to Jesus Christ, you are the greatest gift in my life. You are the anchor to our family and a tremendous wife and mother. You represent everything I want to be as a follower of Jesus. I love you more today than ever, and I am still saying, "You jump, I jump!" I am so glad I get to share this life with you!

My children. Each and every one of you are gifts in my life. You have all been through so much and have endured so well. I admire Brittany's resilience, Caleb's focus, Clayton's passion, Aubrey's tenderness, and the joy Luke and Addi bring. You have all loved and honored Trey so well, and one day we will all be reunited again. I love each of you with all that I have, and I am so proud of you. I love being your dad.

My parents. I would not be where I am today without you. I

am grateful for your influence in my life and the sacrifices you have made. I love you both very much.

My extended family. You mean so much to me. I could say so many things, but at the top of the list is the support you have given. You have all prayed, sacrificed, helped, and served in so many ways. I am beyond thankful for each of you. Toby, Cynthia, Daniel, and Greg, I miss you more than I can say, and I pray this book makes you proud.

My First Baptist Church family in Newcastle, Oklahoma. You are such a gift to me and my family. You have walked with us through the loss of Trey, the hardships with Caleb, and everything in between. From the bottom of my heart, thank you. Thank you for loving me, praying for me, cheering me on, and supporting me. I love you all!

The big "C" Church. Our family has been overwhelmed by the Church. On every part of our journey, we have encountered Christ-followers who have walked with me and my family through some very difficult days. I could never express my love and gratitude to every believer who has ministered to and with us along the way. Many of you prayed for us like you would your own family, and for that, we could never thank you enough. You have been some of God's greatest gifts in our lives. I love you all!

Kevin McAfee and Jennifer Willingham. How do I even begin to thank you both? God brought both of you into our lives at the perfect time and in the perfect way. Kevin, you have encouraged us, believed with us, and sacrificed so much for us. We are so honored to be in your life and know that the best is yet to come. We love you. Jennifer, thank you for being willing to step into our lives. Thank you for listening to the Holy Spirit and following His lead. We are grateful for your investment in us and your belief in how God is using and will use our story. We love you!

The countless doctors and nurses who have helped us along the way, specifically those at Children's Hospital Los Angeles, Medical City Dallas and Texas Oncology, OU Medical, Craig Hospital, and QLI. By the grace of God, we have been cared for by some of the very best doctors, nurses, therapists, hospitals, and facilities along our journey. You will never know the impact you have had on our family, and we are very thankful for each of you. We love you all very much!

Thomas Nelson. Thank you for believing in our story and helping us tell it. We are beyond grateful for you and believe God is going to use this book significantly. We look forward to our continued relationship as we partner together to impact people's lives eternally.

My Lord and Savior, Jesus Christ. I am nothing, have nothing, and can do nothing apart from You. Thank You for saving me as a sixteen-year-old, calling me to ministry, and using me for Your glory! As the psalmist said, "I love you, O LORD, my strength!" You have been so good and faithful in every aspect of my life, and I give You all praise and honor. I pray every single person who reads our story would be drawn to You. Please use it all for Your glory!

The *#butGod*
Seven-Day
Devotional

INTRODUCTION

When Caleb was in the emergency room, Emily and I were not getting any updates on his situation. At some point I walked up to a nurse, pulled her to the side, and said, "Ma'am, can you please give me an update on our son?" I will never forget what happened next. The nurse took me by the hand, looked intently into my eyes, and said, "Sir, your son needs a miracle."

Upon hearing those words, I nearly fell to the floor. I sat down on the ground and, with tears in my eyes, sent a message to my family, staff, and close friends. I told them what the nurse had said, and I ended the message by saying, "but God."

As you read in this book, little did we know how much those two words would mean to us. Every single time someone said Caleb could not do something, we would say "but God." Those two words simply mean that God always has the final say. The Bible has "but God" all over it, and in each instance the truth remains that God, in any and every circumstance, always has the last word.

I pray these seven #butGod devotions will encourage you in your faith and in your journey of knowing and walking with God. There are seven devotions for seven days, and I pray that each one will point you to the reality that God is good, perfect, and in control. He can be fully trusted in life and in death and in everything in-between. Always remember: #butGod.

Day 1

As for you, you meant evil against me, **but**
God *meant it for good, to bring it about that*
many people should be kept alive, as they are
today.

—Genesis 50:20

The life of Joseph is perhaps one of the most powerful
stories in the Bible. Joseph epitomizes trusting God
regardless of life's circumstances. There is much we can
learn from his life.

God gave seventeen-year-old Joseph some unique
dreams. They revealed that one day Joseph would be in
a position of great authority and everyone in his family
would submit to him. When Joseph relayed the dreams to
his family, his brothers grew extremely jealous.

Joseph's brothers developed a plan to harm him. They
stripped him of a coat his father had given him and threw
him into a pit. Not long after, they sold him into slavery
to a group of travelers. The brothers then put the blood of
an animal on Joseph's coat and returned it to their father,

exclaiming that a fierce animal had torn Joseph to pieces and all that remained was his coat.

This began a long journey for Joseph and his family. Joseph ended up in the home of a high-ranking officer of Pharaoh's, a man named Potiphar. Potiphar soon noticed that Joseph was special. In fact the Bible says, "The LORD was with Joseph, and he became a successful man" (Gen. 39:2). Potiphar trusted Joseph completely and put him in charge of his entire household.

Potiphar's wife took notice of Joseph and pursued him day after day. One day she grabbed hold of him but Joseph fled, leaving behind his garment. Potiphar's wife lied to her husband and said that Joseph had tried to lie with her, and Potiphar threw him into prison. The Bible says, "But the LORD was with Joseph and showed him steadfast love and gave him favor in the sight of the keeper of the prison" (Gen. 39:21). God continued to show Himself faithful regardless of Joseph's circumstances.

Two of Joseph's fellow prisoners had dreams and Joseph explained what they meant. One dream resulted in death for one of the inmates, and the other dream resulted in restoration for the other prisoner. When that prisoner was released, Joseph pled with the man not to forget him. The man forgot him. *But God* did not.

I encourage you to read Genesis 41–50 for the rest of Joseph's amazing story filled with *but God* moments.

Joseph placed his life in God's hands and left the results to Him. This is often easy to do when everything is going your way, but it is in the trying times when you discover if you truly love and trust God. This is why the story of Joseph is so spectacular. I am sure Joseph wavered in his faith. I am sure Joseph questioned God at times. I am sure Joseph grieved the loss of time with family. I am sure Joseph was frustrated by being falsely accused.

Yet in all of it, we see that God was with Joseph and Joseph was with God. He knew that God had used all the ups and downs of his life for a greater purpose. He knew that everything he was and had was a result of the goodness and grace of God. This allowed Joseph to stand before his brothers after many years had passed and say, "You meant evil against me, *but God* meant it for good." God always has the final say.

Today, live in that reality. Nothing touches your life that does not first pass through the hands of God. God is with you and is using whatever you are facing for your good and His glory! #butGod.

Day 2

My flesh and my heart may fail, **but God**
is the strength of my heart and my portion
forever.

—PSALM 73:26

The psalms contain some of the most powerful verses in
the Bible. In many ways it is like reading the journals
of some of the heroes of the faith. In fact, if you want to
feel normal about your Christian life, just read the book of
Psalms. If you read five psalms each day, you can read them
all in thirty days, and personally, I think that is a great thing
to do.

You will read phrases similar to the following:

"How long will You forsake me, Lord?"
"How long must I wait for you?"
"Against You and You only have I sinned."
"Have mercy on me according to Your lovingkindness."
"The Lord is my light and salvation; whom shall I fear?"
"Great is the Lord and greatly to be praised."

In one psalm the writer wonders where God is, and in another he praises God for His faithfulness. This is what much of our Christian lives look like. Some days we find ourselves reveling in the nearness of God; other days we feel like God is nowhere to be found. This is when we must remember who God is and focus on Him instead of on our feelings or circumstances. Our perspective is largely shaped by our view of God, and our view must be derived from the truth of God's Word.

Psalm 73 delivers some powerful truths: "Whom have I in heaven but you? And there is nothing on earth that I desire besides you" (v. 25). The psalmist wrote that he is nothing apart from God. He knew that God was his strength and help. He understood that without God he had nothing. This why at the end of the psalm he said, "But for me it is good to be near God; I have made the Lord GOD my refuge" (v. 28). This truth is critical to embrace in our hard world. We must draw near to God, for He is the only true constant in our lives. As I frequently say, "Life is often not good, but God is always good."

After the psalmist declared his need for God, he wrote, "My flesh and my heart may fail, *but God* is the strength of my heart and my portion forever" (v. 26). There are those two words again: *but God*.

This is what it means and looks like to live totally dependent on God. He is not interested in those who desire to show Him how strong they are. Rather, He looks for the weak to show Himself as strong. Isn't that what the apostle Paul discovered in his journey with God? Paul had a thorn in his flesh that he begged God to remove, yet God let it remain. Paul learned to say, "I will boast all the more gladly of my weaknesses, so that the power of Christ may rest upon me . . . for when I am weak, then I am strong" (2 Cor. 12:9–10).

God is attracted to weakness, for it is in our weakness that we look beyond ourselves to Him. Suffering and hardship have a way of doing what nothing else can: they cause us to look beyond ourselves. The psalmist captured this perfectly as he declared that his heart and flesh will indeed fail, but his strength and hope are not in himself, they are in "but God."

Today let your weakness, suffering, pain, heartache, frustration—anything—cause you to turn your heart to the only One who can help you. Instead of resenting your life, embrace it and live for the glory of God. Always remember, God has the final say. Trust Him!

Day 3

And he said to them, "You are those who
*justify yourselves before men, **but God** knows*
your hearts. For what is exalted among men is
an abomination in the sight of God."
—LUKE 16:15

God is always most concerned with the heart. "For the LORD sees not as man sees; man looks on the outward appearance, but the LORD looks on the heart" (1 Sam. 16:7). This is one of the things that made Jesus' presence on the earth so powerful. He knew if someone truly trusted Him—or just appeared to.

Jesus was harshest with the religious leaders. They wanted to appear different than they were. Instead of helping people find God, they often made the path to God more difficult. They loved to stand on the street corners and say prayers and tout their biblical knowledge for others to see. They loved to appear as though they were generous and cared for the poor. In reality they were "like whitewashed tombs, which outwardly appear beautiful, but within are full of dead people's bones and all uncleanness" (Matt. 23:27). In other words, they were phonies. They had everyone fooled except God.

Jesus often told stories, and the point of His stories was to make a truth-connection to people's hearts. It is beautiful to read about tax collectors, adulterers, liars, thieves, and so forth, repenting of their sins and trusting in Jesus. But not everyone responded that way to Jesus. The religious leaders were extremely critical of who He claimed to be, what He said, and what He did. They hated that He spent time with sinners. But the Bible says He came "to seek and to save the lost" (Luke 19:10).

Jesus, 100 percent man and 100 percent God, not only saw the religious leaders' physical presence, He also saw their spiritual condition. In Luke 16, Jesus had just said, "No servant can serve two masters, for either he will hate the one and love the other, or he will be devoted to the one and despise the other. You cannot serve God and money" (v. 13). Knowing that the religious leaders were lovers of money, Jesus directed His next statement right at their hearts: "You are those who justify yourselves before men, *but God* knows your hearts. For what is exalted among men is an abomination in the sight of God" (v. 15).

Jesus was proving to these men that He knew what was inside them. In other words, they could fool man, but they could not fool God. God knew their hearts and even though they were often exalted before men, it was not men they would ultimately stand before; it was God.

This is a great reminder for us that we are to live for an audience of one. As Jesus would later say, "For what does it profit a man to gain the whole world and forfeit his soul?" (Mark 8:36). What matters most in this life is humbling ourselves like children, admitting we have sinned, and entrusting our lives entirely into God's care. God did not reject the religious leaders because they were sinners but because they were too prideful to admit they were sinners.

Today, remember that God knows your heart. You may have everyone fooled but God. Stop trying to be someone you are not. Admit your need for God. Confess that you have fallen short. Ask God to help you. Place all your hope and trust in Jesus. Stop worrying about what people think about you, and concern yourself only with what God thinks about you. He loves you. He died for you. He rose from the dead to give you true life. This is why He gets the final say over you, but you must turn your whole self over to Him. Why? #butGod.

Day 4

But God *chose what is foolish in the world to*
shame the wise; God chose what is weak in
the world to shame the strong.
—1 CORINTHIANS 1:27

"N ot to us, O LORD, not to us, but to your name give
glory" (Psalm 115:1). Twice the psalmist says "not to
us." He understood that his existence was to give glory to
the only One worthy of it. Scripture says over and over that
if we boast, we are to boast in the Lord. We exist for God.
God does not exist for us.

If you study the Bible, you will see that God has a
different way of doing things. Man is all about picking the
smartest, strongest, and most attractive, but God often
does the opposite. I can remember being on the playground
during recess, and when the time would come to choose
teams, the best players always got picked first.

That mentality is engrained in mankind. We think the
people God uses will be like the people the world would
choose. Thankfully, this is not the case. God likes to take

weak people, who yield themselves fully to Him, and use them to do incredible things. Not so they get the glory, but so that He does. God likes to select people the world would not pick and display His power through them.

One example is the apostle Paul. Paul may have appeared to be strong in man's eyes, but in reality he was weak. God appeared to Paul on the road to Damascus and temporarily blinded him. God got Paul's attention and radically changed him. Paul became one of the greatest missionaries and church planters the world has ever known, along with writing much of the New Testament. God did this, and He got the glory.

The church at Corinth had many problems, but Paul loved the people and longed to see them walk with Jesus in purity and power. When he wrote them, he reminded them of his weakness. He said,

> And I was with you in weakness and in fear and much trembling, and my speech and my message were not in plausible words of wisdom, but in demonstration of the Spirit and of power, so that your faith might not rest in the wisdom of men but in the power of God. (1 Cor. 2:3–5)

What powerful words! Paul was saying, "Not to me, not to me, but to God be the glory."

Imagine your life being like a simple baseball glove. The glove has no power until a hand goes into the glove, and then the glove does whatever the hand tells it to do. That is like you and me. We are powerless without the power of God. On our own, we are nothing but empty gloves. But when God fills our lives, He uses us in unimaginable ways. When Christ comes to dwell in our hearts through faith, He changes us. He empowers us. He strengthens us. Not for our glory, but for His.

Today, recognize your weakness and rejoice in His strength. He has chosen to use you. He has gifted you. He has called you. He has empowered you. He has done all these things and so much more, that you might be used in ways beyond yourself and bring glory to His name. Do not focus on you, focus on Him, and watch what He will do in your life. God can do so much more with a weak servant dependent on Him than with a strong, self-dependent person. This is what #butGod is all about, and it's all about Him!

Day 5

But God, *being rich in mercy, because of the*
great love with which he loved us.
—EPHESIANS 2:4

The word *gospel* literally means "good news." Everyone
loves good news. We especially love good news after
we have received bad news. Think of the doctor who walks
into the hospital room and says, "Bad news, you're sick. But
the good news is, I am going to prescribe a medication that
will make you better." All of a sudden, the bad news is swallowed by the good news. Good news changes everything.

When we think about the gospel, we must think of both
bad news and good news. In his letter to the Ephesians, the
apostle Paul began by delivering the bad news:

And you were dead in the trespasses and sins in which
you once walked, following the course of this world, following the prince of the power of the air, the spirit that is
now at work in the sons of disobedience—among whom
we all once lived in the passions of our flesh, carrying out

the desires of the body and the mind, and were by nature children of wrath, like the rest of mankind. (Eph. 2:1–3)

This is not just bad news, it is the worst news. These verses describe the condition of every human being who has ever lived or will ever live on the planet. Left to ourselves, we are hopeless. It is as if the doctor walked in the room and said, "Bad news, you're not just sick. You're dying, and there is nothing that can be done."

But in the very next verse in Ephesians, two powerful words change everything. Paul wrote, *"But God*, being rich in mercy, because of the great love with which he loved us, even when we were dead in our trespasses, made us alive together with Christ" (vv. 4–5). *But God!* Those words are beautiful and transforming, and they deliver the good news to us. This time, the doctor says, "Bad news, you're dying. Good news, I have a cure." All of a sudden the bad news is swallowed up in good news, all because of the truth of #butGod.

The gospel reminds us that our sin does not need to have the final say in our lives. We can look to our Creator and Savior and find forgiveness, healing, and life. Jesus said, "Truly, truly, I say to you, whoever hears my word and believes him who sent me has eternal life. He does not come into judgment, but has passed from death to life" (John 5:24). That is the power of #butGod. We were dead in our sins, without hope, but God did not abandon us there. He entered the brokenness and chaos of this world and rescued sinners from themselves. He provided a way to pass from death to life. Why? Because He is rich in mercy. Because He is a good God who loves to redeem and restore. Because He refused to let sin and death have the final say. Because He gets glory from bringing people from death to life.

All of the gospel can be summed up in these two words: *but God*. Have you embraced the gospel? Have you trusted Jesus? Have you experienced #butGod? If not, you can. Call out to the One who created you. Confess your sin and your need for forgiveness. Surrender your heart and life to Jesus. When you do, you will find all that you have desperately been searching for. You will be changed by the only One who is rich in mercy and who is mighty to save.

Day 6

> But God *shows his love for us in that while*
> *we were still sinners, Christ died for us.*
> —ROMANS 5:8

How do you know if someone truly loves you? Is it by what they say or what they do? What a person says is important, but what they do is even more important. If their actions do not back up their words, then their words become meaningless. The age-old expression is true: "Actions speak louder than words."

God's Word says many things, and behind every word are His faithful and perfect actions. All of God's words are true. The moment He makes a promise, He keeps that promise. He is never early or late, and He is faithful 100 percent of the time. His Word never returns void, and what He says always comes to pass. He is the embodiment of truth, always acting with sovereign grace and perfect love.

Perhaps nothing shows this more than the person and work of Jesus Christ. Hundreds of prophecies foretold a Messiah would come, and He did. It was said the Messiah would be sinless, and He was. It was declared that the Savior of the world would suffer and die, and He did. Jesus Christ came into the world as the perfect fulfillment of God's redemptive plan, and He exemplified God's sacrificial love for mankind. As the most famous verse in the Bible says, "For God so loved the world, that he gave his only Son" (John 3:16). God proved His love for us by doing what He said He would do. Jesus Christ is the evidence of how loving and faithful God is; through Him the Word became flesh, and God's word became action.

Romans 5:8 declares that God did not just say He loved us, He proved it. "*But God* shows His love for us in that while we were still sinners, Christ died for us." Isn't that beautiful? While we were still sinners, Christ died for us. Think of it this way:

> *but God showed He loved us when we were unlovable.*
> *but God showed He loved us when we ran from Him.*
> *but God showed He loved us when we rejected Him.*
> *but God showed He loved us when we trusted in things other than Him.*

The list could go on and on, but the message is clear. *But God* showed His love for us, period. We did not deserve His love. We could not earn His love. He simply gave it. When you and I understand this reality, it is a game changer for our lives. When we realize who we are and what we deserve apart from Jesus, we are forever humbled and grateful for the words *but God*. Because of those two words, we can never be the same. In light of this life-altering truth, read these words from the beloved hymn "The Love of God":

The love of God is greater far, than tongue or pen can ever tell;
It goes beyond the highest star and reaches to the lowest hell.
The guilty pair, bowed down with care,
God gave His Son to win;
His erring child He reconciled and pardoned from his sin.[1]

Never forget, God did not just say He loves us, He proved it. He died for us and the only fitting response can be that we live for Him.

Day 7

But God raised Him from the dead.
—ACTS 13:30

There are so many important events in Jesus' life. Among them are the virgin birth, His sinless life, the crucifixion, and the resurrection. Honestly, each one of those events is crucial. If you were to remove any one of them, the validity of Christianity would crumble.

But the resurrection of Jesus is the capstone. As the apostle Paul wrote,

And if Christ has not been raised, then our preaching is in vain and your faith is in vain. We are even found to be misrepresenting God, because we testified about God that he raised Christ. . . . And if Christ has not been raised, your faith is futile and you are still in your sins. Then those also who have fallen asleep in Christ have perished. If in Christ we have hope in this life only, we are of all people most to be pitied. (1 Cor. 15:14–15, 17–19)

Think of the power of these words: If Christ had not been raised from the dead, then we of all people are to be most pitied. I can't emphasize enough the importance of Jesus' resurrection. Without it we would still be dead in our sin and left without hope. The good news is, although Jesus died He did not stay dead, *"but God* raised Him from the dead"* (Acts 13:30). The resurrection proved once and for all that sin and death do not have the final say. God does.

When Jesus walked on the earth, He was both loved and hated. Strangely, the people who hated Him most were the religious leaders. They did not like that He claimed to be the Messiah. He came into the world as a suffering servant instead of as the conquering king they wanted.

The religious leaders resented Jesus because they knew only God could forgive sins, and when Jesus declared that He forgave someone's sin, He was asserting His divinity, that He *was* God. But as much as they hated Him, they could not deny His incredible power. He was healing the sick, driving our demons, and raising the dead. With every miracle Jesus performed, the religious leaders hated Him even more.

They believed that the only way to get rid of Jesus was to kill Him, so they had Him arrested, falsely accused, and sentenced to death on a cross. But this was all part of God's redemptive plan. Jesus' life was not taken; it was laid down, and it was laid down because God so loved the world, even those who plotted against Him.

The religious leaders thought they had won.

"*But God* raised Him from the dead." Three days later, the greatest miracle of all time happened, showing that Christ was indeed the King of kings and Lord of lords. A declaration once and for all that God has the final word over death and the grave and over every single thing in this life and eternity. Jesus said, "I am the resurrection and the life. Whoever believes in me, though he die, yet shall he live, and everyone who lives and believes in me shall never die" (John 11:25–26). Jesus is the only way. He is the embodiment of God's promise fulfilled. He is the hope for yesterday, today, and forever. He is #butGod!

Commonly Asked Questions

Does Caleb remember anything about the wreck? What was his last memory before the wreck and first memory waking up?

Caleb doesn't remember anything about the wreck or the events surrounding the wreck. His last memory is from about a month before the accident. He also doesn't have a clear first memory of waking up.

Everything with Caleb has been a process. As he woke up from the coma, he slowly began to be able to communicate about the past and present.

Could Caleb hear anything while he was in the coma?

Caleb says that he doesn't remember hearing anything while in the coma for eight weeks. However, on the day he "woke up," his speech therapist began asking him questions. Some of these questions were specifically about Caleb's situation, and he knew the answers. He couldn't use words early on, but he could point to answers on a flip chart. He knew he had been in a wreck, he knew he was in Colorado in a rehabilitation hospital, he knew his age, he knew the date. Even though Caleb doesn't remember hearing things in his coma, he was clearly processing and retaining information.

What was Caleb like before the wreck, and how is he different now?

Caleb was quiet and shy before the wreck. He had a small group of friends that he was more funny and bold with, but for the most part he was introverted, easily embarrassed, and shy.

After the wreck, Caleb has become very bold, outgoing, extroverted, and funny. The quiet boldness he had before the wreck has become a very public boldness. Caleb loves all people. He loves talking to people, sharing his story with people, encouraging people, and praying with people. He is 100 percent different and is such a powerful witness for Jesus and a true joy to observe and spend time with.

If Caleb could go back to December 19, 2017, would he change anything?

Caleb is very quick to say no. Caleb says, "When I look at the direction my life was headed and where it is now, how could I want to go back?" He believes the wreck did not flip his life upside down but rather flipped it in the right direction. From the very beginning, Caleb has consistently said he would not change a thing. He believes God has spared his life and has left him on this earth for a specific purpose.

What are the things most difficult for Caleb now?

Caleb struggles with several physical things. He battles a condition called ataxia, which is simply part of his brain injury. It makes doing anything involving fine motor skills very difficult. Writing, putting in his contacts—normal daily tasks—are all challenges.

He still struggles with balance and coordination. Caleb can walk, and even run some, but it is very difficult for him. Caleb's speech is good, but it can also be a challenge to understand at times.

He battles vision problems that cause him difficulty when it comes to focusing. He can't drive a vehicle, although he sometimes drives a golf cart.

Caleb's long-term memory is good, but he sometimes struggles with remembering simple things such as what time to be somewhere. All in all, Caleb is a walking, talking, and living miracle. His focus, perspective, and attitude have never been stronger. In all things that matter most, Caleb is doing amazing!

What keeps Caleb motivated on a daily basis? How does he stay encouraged and positive?

Caleb is a rare combination of contentment and motivation. He recently memorized the entire book of Philippians, and his favorite verse is Philippians 4:11, which says, "For I have learned in whatever situation I am to be content."

Caleb uses the phrase "It's a snare to compare." He realizes that others have it easier than he does, and some have it harder. His theme is simply to embrace the life God has given him and use it for God's glory. Caleb stays content and motivated by reading and memorizing God's Word and by worshipping. Caleb listens to worship music and sermons all the time, and those things keep his mind and perspective right. He also does physical exercise, works on his speech and handwriting, and does whatever therapy he can to improve. He is always ready and willing to work hard.

What is the greatest miracle God has done in Caleb's life?

Caleb says that the physical restoration, even though it is not 100 percent, is amazing, but the greatest miracle is what has happened in his heart. He says he has been changed from the inside out and is a completely new person. He says that God took someone who should have died and has now made him really live. Caleb would say he is more alive now than he ever has been.

If you could tell people only one thing from your journey, what would you tell them?

Caleb encourages everyone to make sure they have a relationship with Jesus. He knows that life can change at any moment and you must be ready to both meet the Lord and live for the Lord no matter your circumstances. Caleb would say, "Don't wait for something bad to happen to get your attention. Start living for Jesus right now. He is worth it."

Songs That Have Inspired Us Along the Way

"Battle Belongs," Phil Wickham

"Because He Lives," Carrie Underwood

"Christ Be Magnified," Cody Carnes

"Even If," Kutless

"Even If," MercyMe

"God of Miracles," Chris McClarney

"God of Revival," Phil Wickham

"God's Not Done with You," Tauren Wells

"Goodness of God," Bethel Music, Jenn Johnson

"Here Again," Elevation Worship

"His Name is Jesus," Phil Wickham

"Homesick," MercyMe

"How Great Thou Art," Carrie Underwood

"Resurrecting," Elevation Worship

"The Reason for the World," Matthew West

"Until Grace," Tauren Wells

"Way Maker," Leeland

"We Praise You," Bethel Music, Brandon Lake

"Worthy of Your Name," Passion Worship, Sean
   Curran

The #butGod Movement

Six months after Caleb's accident, he was introduced to Kevin McAfee by mutual friends. Kevin would produce a feature film that documented Caleb's miraculous healing and recovery. The documentary featured several Oklahoma basketball athletes who would later turn professional. Included with the basketball players was the OU basketball head coach, Lon Kruger. From police officers to first responders, medical doctors and on-the-scene medical vehicle professionals, groups of people shared of how their lives had been changed. Many shared stories of what happened that rainy night in December.

Caleb continued to share his #butGod story in Oklahoma, and the momentum grew, with churches around the country inviting Caleb and our family to speak. At those events we used and we're still using footage from the documentary to help share the vision with groups, churches, and businesses. The goal is to inspire people to share their #butGod stories.

The power of a #butGod testimony is like none other. Eighteen months after the accident, the impact of #butGod was beginning to grow. In October 2019, Lester Holt and the *NBC Nightly News* crew shared the miracle of Caleb running his first 5K in his senior year of high school. Before the accident Caleb ran a 5K in seventeen minutes; this 5K took him fifty-one minutes and ten seconds. Two weeks in a row, the NBC network followed Caleb in his miraculous recovery apex, bringing one more *Inspiring America* story to our nation.

Churches continue to reach out to our family, and we are responding as fast as humanly possible to meet the need. Our desire is to inspire people everywhere to share their #butGod stories.

Please join us in praying for a #butGod movement that will sweep across this nation and change the world.

Notes

Prologue

1. Tauren Wells, Here Again (live)—Tauren Wells,"
   live performance posted on February 20, 2019,
   YouTube video, 4:25–6:01, https://www.youtube.com
   /watch?v=d3pGYeo0_yY.

Chapter 8: The Long, Winding Road

1. "Brain Injury Rehabilitation," Craig Hospital, accessed
   December 29, 2021, https://craighospital.org/programs
   /traumatic-brain-injury.

Chapter 9: The Tortoise Becomes the Hare

1. "'It's Only God and No One Else,' Newcastle Teen
   Defies the Odds," Oklahoma News 4, April 24, 2018,
   https://kfor.com/news/its-only-god-and-no-one-else/.

Chapter 14: Never Give Up, Never Give In, Never Let Go

1. C. S. Lewis, *The Problem of Pain* (1940; repr., New York:
   HarperOne, 2015), 91.
2. Leah MarieAnn Klett, "Joni Eareckson Tada Reveals
   'First Thing' She'll Do in Heaven: 'It Will Be My Joy and
   Sacrifice,'" *The Christian Post*, September 15, 2019,

https://www.christianpost.com/news/joni-eareckson-tada
-reveals-first-thing-shell-do-in-heaven-it-will-be-my-joy
-and-sacrifice.html.

3. Personal conversation with Randy Alcorn.

The *#butGod* Seven-Day Devotional
1. Frederick M. Lehman, "The Love of God," (1917),
   Hymnary.org, accessed June 13, 2022, https://hymnary.org
   /text/the_love_of_god_is_greater_far.

About the Author

Jeremy Freeman is lead pastor at First Baptist Church in Newcastle, Oklahoma. He is a sought-after speaker for inspirational events hosted by churches, conventions, conferences, businesses, and schools. He writes regularly at his blog site PastorJFreeman.com. Jeremy, his wife, Emily, and their six children live in Newcastle, Oklahoma.